ACT V

DEDICATION

TO THE REV. H. CARD, M.A. F.R.S. F.A.S. ETC. ETC. ETC.

My DEAR SIR,

As you have, in a late publication, which displays your usual learning and judgment, mentioned this performance in terms, perhaps dictated by friendship rather than critical impartiality, I must beg to inscribe it to your name.

There are many prejudices with which a playwright has to contend, on his first appearance, more especially if he court the reader in lieu of the spectator; and it is so great an effort to give up any established topic of condolement, that we can hardly yet expect those, who call themselves "the critics," to abandon their favourite complaint of the degeneracy which characterizes the efforts of contemporary tragic writers. But let any unprejudiced person turn to the productions even of the present year; let him candidly examine the anonymous Play, "The Court of Tuscany," and compare its best scenes with the master-pieces of Rowe or Otway; let him peruse Allan Cunningham's poetical drama, which has won the applause of the highest literary authority of the day; let him dwell upon the energetic grandeur and warlike animation which Croly has so successfully displayed in pourtraying the restless spirit of Catiline; and I think his verdict will place this age not the last among those which have done honour to the British stage.

These instances are sufficient to attest the flourishing condition of dramatic literature, but, alas! we must seek them in the closet, not in their proper home, the populous theatre, for there we shall meet with a sight, sufficient to deter the boldest adventurer from hazarding the representation of his best and most vaunted piece, our countrymen barely enduring the poetry of Shakspeare as the vehicle of a fashionable song or a gaudy pageant. Even the theatre itself however may appear "not yet enslaved, not wholly vile," as long as the classic taste of Milman, the plaintive sweetness of Barry Cornwall, and the frank nature of Knowles, linger, like flowers upon the Muse's grave. But they have almost deserted the public haunt, and England can hardly boast anything that deserves to be called a national stage.

The following scenes were written, as you well know, exclusively for the closet, founded upon facts, which occurred at Oxford, and are well detailed and illustrated by an interesting ballad in a little volume of Poems, lately published at Oxford, entitled the Midland Minstrel, by Mr. Gillet: and may thus be succinctly narrated.

The Manciple of one of the Colleges early in the last century had a very beautiful daughter, who was privately married to a student without the knowledge of the parents on either side.

During the long vacation subsequent to this union the husband was introduced to a young lady, who was at the same time proposed as his bride: absence, the fear of his father's displeasure, the presence of a lovely object, and, most likely, a natural fickleness of disposition overcame any regard he might have cherished for his ill-fated wife, and finally he became deeply enamoured of her unconscious rival. In the contest of duties and desires, which was the consequence of this passion, the worse part of man prevailed, and he formed and executed a design almost unparalleled in the annals of crime.

His second nuptials were at hand when he returned to Oxford, and to her who was now an obstacle to his happiness. Late at night he prevailed upon his victim to accompany him to a lone spot in the Divinity Walk, and there murdered and buried her. The wretch escaped detection, and the horrid deed remained unknown till he confessed it on his death-bed. The remains of the unfortunate girl were dug up in the place described, and the Divinity Walk was deserted and demolished, as haunted ground. Such are the outlines of a Minor's Tragedy.

My age, it will be said, is a bad excuse for the publication of a faulty poem; be it so: secure of your approbation, I can meet with a careless smile the frown of him who reads only to condemn.

I am, my dear Sir,
Your's most sincerely,
THOMAS LOVELL BEDDOES.

PERSONS REPRESENTED
The DUKE
LORD ERNEST
HESPERUS, his Son
ORLANDO
CLAUDIO
MORDRED
HUBERT
A HUNTSMAN
BOY, Page to Orlando
JAILOR

OLIVIA, Sister to Orlando
VIOLETTA, her Companion
LENORA, Wife of Mordred
FLORIBEL, her Daughter

Lords, Citizens, Attendants, Guards, &c.

THE BRIDES' TRAGEDY

ACT I

The Brides' Tragedy by Thomas Lovell Beddoes

Thomas Lovell Beddoes was born in Clifton, Bristol on 30th June 1803, the son of Dr. Thomas and Anna Beddoes. He was a radical doctor, known for his pioneering use of nitrous oxide and a friend to Samuel Taylor Coleridge, and she was the sister of the noted novelist Maria Edgeworth

Beddoes was five when his father died but had lived his early years surrounded by the tools and tables of his father's trade.

The next chapter in his life was spent in the comfortable and literary circle of his mother's family. The medical and the literary were the two big influences in his career and clashed in alarming ways causing him to develop a macabre and deep interest in death.

He was educated at Charterhouse school before proceeding to Pembroke College, Oxford, in 1820. It was during his time at Oxford that he wrote and published his poetry volume 'The Improvisatore' (1821), which he afterwards attempted to withdraw from the market.

The following year he published his well-reviewed blank-verse drama called 'The Bride's Tragedy' (1822).

In 1824 Beddoes moved to London and befriended the remainder of Shelley's circle and others who would have a marked influence on his life.

He returned to Oxford for his B.A. examinations, but, hearing that his mother had been taken ill in Florence immediately left for Italy. Sadly, by the time he arrived his mother was dead.

All accounts of Beddoes attest that his fascination with the dead, with all its rituals and occult shadowing, was marked and pronounced. He continued to write but it now takes a darker, more macabre form. His attempts at writing plays quickly fall away, his poetry seems to reflect much of his inner fears and outlook in an intense and lyrical way with voluptuous horror that is uniquely expressed.

Beddoes again returned to Oxford for his exams in 1825 but seems to have taken the decision at this point to remove himself from sight.

He now spent the next four years at the medical school at the Hanoverian university of Göttingen, pursuing both academic excellence and personal behavior that was so appalling he was eventually asked to leave. Beddoes moved location to the medical school in the Bavarian university of Würzburg and received his doctorate in 1831. By now he had also developed a passion for liberationist politics resulting in his writing many anti-establishment pamphlets, the upshot of which was his expulsion from the country by the Bavarian government in 1832.

Switzerland now became his new home. Beddoes promoted liberal causes until the political winds changed in Zürich and he left in 1839 and was back in England by the following summer. But traction in any direction was proving difficult for him.

He was back in Basel, Switzerland by 1844 and the curtain was fast drawing on his life. Despite a return to England in 1846 his behavior was becoming both wild and uncontrollable. A relationship with Konrad

Degen, a baker with designs on a career as a playwright, did nothing to persuade the opinions of others that he was descending into lunacy.

Accounts now suggest that his health began to fail after coming into contact with a diseased cadaver in Frankfurt. Beddoes attempted suicide but the botched attempt resulted in gangrene and a partial amputation of the leg in October 1848.

In January 1849, Beddoes wrote to his sister professing that his physical state was due to a riding accident. At some point he now obtained a measure of the poison curare.

Thomas Lovell Beddoes died in on 26th January 1849. He was 45. A note found here described him as "food for what I am good for—worms."

For more than 20 years before his death he had worked on 'Death's Jest Book', which was published posthumously in 1850, it also included a memoir by T. F. Kelsall. This was very well received and is often regarded as a classic. His Collected Poems were published in 1851.

As a dramatist his later works received criticism but his poems were "full of thought and richness of diction", and as "masterpieces of intense feeling exquisitely expressed".

Index of Contents

A Garden

HESPERUS [alone]
Now Eve has strewn the sun's wide billowy couch
With rosered feathers moulted from her wing,
Still scanty-sprinkled clouds, like lagging sheep,
Some golden-fleeced, some streaked with delicate pink,
Are creeping up the welkin, and behind
The wind, their boisterous shepherd, whistling drives them,
From the drear wilderness of night to drink
Antipodean noon. At such a time,
While to wild melody fantastic dreams
Dance their gay morrice in the midmost air,
And sleepers' truant fancies fly to join them;
While that winged song, the restless nightingale
Turns her sad heart to music, sweet it is
Unseen on, the moss-cushioned sward to lean,
And into some coy ear pour out the soul
In sighs and whispers.

[Enter **FLORIBEL**.

So late, Floribel?
Nay, since I see that arch smile on thy cheek
Rippling so prettily, I will not chide,
Although the breeze and I have sighed for you
A dreary while, and the veiled Moon's mild eye
Has long been seeking for her loveliest nymph.
Come, come, my love, or shall I call you bride?

FLORIBEL
E'en what you will, so that you hold me dear.

HESPERUS
Well, both my love and bride; see, here's a bower
Of eglantine with honeysuckles woven,
Where not a spark of prying light creeps in,
So closely do the sweets enfold each other.
'Tis Twilight's home; come in, my gentle love,
And talk to me. So! I've a rival here;
What's this that sleeps so sweetly on your neck?

FLORIBEL
Jealous so soon, my Hesperus? Look then,
It is a bunch of flowers I pulled for you:
Here's the blue violet, like Pandora's eye,

When first it darkened with immortal life.

HESPERUS
Sweet as thy lips. Fie on those taper fingers,
Have they been brushing the long grass aside
To drag the daisy from it's hiding-place,
Where it shuns light, the Danäe of flowers,
With gold up-hoarded on its virgin lap?

FLORIBEL
And here's a treasure that I found by chance,
A lily of the valley; low it lay
Over a mossy mound, withered and weeping
As on a fairy's grave.

HESPERUS
Of all the posy
Give me the rose, though there's a tale of blood
Soiling its name. In elfin annals old
'Tis writ, how Zephyr, envious of his love,
(The love he bare to Summer, who since then
Has weeping visited the world;) once found
The baby Perfume cradled in a violet;
('Twas said the beauteous bantling was the child
Of a gay bee, that in his wantonness
Toyed with a peabud in a lady's garland;)
The felon winds, confederate with him,
Bound the sweet slumberer with golden chains,
Pulled from the wreathed laburnum, and together
Deep cast him in the bosom of a rose,
And fed the fettered wretch with dew and air.
At length his soul, that was a lover's sigh,
Waned from his body, and the guilty blossom
His heart's blood stained. The twilight-haunting gnat
His requiem whined, and harebells tolled his knell;
And still the bee, in pied velvet dight,
With melancholy song, from flower to flower,
Goes seeking his lost offspring.

FLORIBEL
Take it then,
In its green sheath. What guess you, Hesperus,
I dreamed last night? Indeed it makes me sad,
And yet I think you love me.

HESPERUS
By the planet
That sheds its tender blue on lovers' sleeps,

Thou art my sweetest, nay, mine only thought:
And when my heart forgets thee, may yon heaven
Forget to guard me.

FLORIBEL
Aye, I knew thou didst;
Yet surely mine's a sad and lonely fate
Thus to be wed to secresy; I doubt,
E'en while I know my doubts are causeless torments.
Yet I conjure thee, if indeed I hold
Some share in thy affections, cast away
The blank and ugly vizor of concealment,
And, if mine homely breeding do not shame thee,
Let thy bride share her noble father's blessing.

HESPERUS
In truth I will; nay, prithee let me kiss
That naughty tear away; I will, by heaven;
For, though austere and old, my sire must gaze
On thy fair innocence with glad forgiveness.
Look up, my love,
See how yon orb, dressed out in all her beams,
Puts out the common stars, and sails along
The stately Queen of heaven; so shall thy beauties,
But the rich casket of a noble soul,
Shine on the world and bless it. Tell me now
This frightful vision.

FLORIBEL
You will banter me;
But I'm a simple girl, and oftentimes
In solitude am very, very mournful:
And now I think how silly 'twas to weep
At such an harmless thing: well, you shall hear.
'Twas on a fragrant bank I laid me down,
Laced o'er and o'er with verdant tendrils, full
Of dark-red strawberries. Anon there came
On the wind's breast a thousand tiny noises,
Like flowers' voices, if they could but speak;
Then slowly did they blend in one sweet strain,
Melodiously divine; and buoyed the soul
Upon their undulations. Suddenly,
Methought, a cloud swam swanlike o'er the sky,
And gently kissed the earth, a fleecy nest,
With roses, rifled from the cheek of Morn,
Sportively strewn; upon the ethereal couch,
Her fair limbs blending with the enamoured mist,
Lovely above the portraiture of words,

In beauteous languor lay the Queen of Smiles:
In tangled garlands, like a golden haze,
Or fay-spun threads of light, her locks were floating,
And in their airy folds slumbered her eyes,
Dark as the nectar-grape that gems the vines
In the bright orchard of the Hesperides.
Within the ivory cradle of her breast
Gambolled the urchin god, with saucy hand
Dimpling her cheeks, or sipping eagerly
The rich ambrosia of her melting lips:
Beneath them swarmed a bustling mob of Loves,
Tending the sparrow stud, or with bees' wings
Imping their arrows. Here stood one alone,
Blowing a pyre of blazing lovers' hearts
With bellows full of absence-caused sighs:
Near him his work-mate mended broken vows
With dangerous gold, or strung soft rhymes together
Upon a lady's tress. Some swelled their cheeks,
Like curling rose-leaves, or the red wine's bubbles,
In petulant debate, gallantly tilting
Astride their darts. And one there was alone,
Who with wet downcast eyelids threw aside
The remnants of a broken heart, and looked
Into my face and bid me 'ware of love,
Of fickleness, and woe, and mad despair.

HESPERUS
Aye, so he said; and did my own dear girl
Deem me a false one for this foolish dream?
I wish I could be angry: hide, distrustful,
Those penitent blushes in my breast, while I
Sing you a silly song old nurses use
To hush their crying babes with. Tenderly
'Twill chide you.

Song
Poor old pilgrim Misery,
Beneath the silent moon he sate,
A-listening to the screech owl's cry,
And the cold wind's goblin prate
Beside him lay his staff of yew
With withered willow twined,
His scant grey hair all wet with dew,
His cheeks with grief ybrined;
And his cry it was ever, alack!
Alack, and woe is me!

Anon a wanton imp astray

His piteous moaning hears,
And from his bosom steals away
His rosary of tears:
With his plunder fled that urchin elf,
And hid it in your eyes,
Then tell me back the stolen pelf,
Give up the lawless prize;
Or your cry shall be ever, alack!
Alack, and woe is me!

HESPERUS
Not yet asleep?

FLORIBEL
Asleep! No, I could ever,
Heedless of times and seasons, list to thee.
But now the chilly breeze is sallying out
Of dismal clouds; and silent midnight walks
Wrapt in her mourning robe. I fear it's time
To separate.

HESPERUS
So quickly late! oh cruel, spiteful hours,
Why will ye wing your steeds from happiness,
And put a leaden drag upon your wheels
When grief hangs round our hearts. Soon will we meet,
And to part never more.

FLORIBEL
Oh! that dear never,
It will pay all. Good night, and think of me.

HESPERUS
Good night, my love; may music-winged sleep
Bind round thy temples with her poppy wreath;
Soft slumbers to thee.

[Exeunt.

SCENE II

A Room in Orlando's Palace

CLAUDIO and **ORLANDO** meeting.

ORLANDO

Thanks for thy speed, good Claudio; is all done
As I have ordered?

CLAUDIO
Could I be unwilling
In the performance of what you command,
I'd say with what regret I led Lord Ernest
Into the prison. My dear lord,
He was your father's friend—

ORLANDO
And he is mine.
You must not think Orlando so forgetful
As to abuse the reverence of age,
An age, like his, of piety and virtue;
'Tis but a fraud of kindness, sportive force.

CLAUDIO
You joy me much, for now I dare to own
I almost thought it was a cruel deed.

ORLANDO
Nay, you shall hear. The sums he owed my father,
Of which his whole estate is scarce a fourth,
Are never to be claimed, if Hesperus,
His son, be wedded to Olivia. Now
This Hesperus, you tell me, is a votary,
A too much favoured votary of my goddess,
The Dian of our forests, Floribel;
Therefore I use this show of cruelty,
To scare a rival and to gain a brother.

CLAUDIO
Now by the patches on the cheek of the moon,
(Is't not a pretty oath?) a good romance;
We'll have't in ballad metre, with a burthen
Of sighs, how one bright glance of a brown damsel
Lit up the tinder of Orlando's heart
In a hot blaze.

ORLANDO
Enough to kindle up
An altar in my breast! 'Twas but a moment,
And yet I would not sell that grain of time
For thy eternity of heartlessness.

CLAUDIO
Well, well. I can bear nonsense from a lover;

Oh, I've been mad threescore and eighteen times
And three quarters; written twenty yards, two nails,
An inch and a quarter, cloth measure, of sonnets;
Wasted as much salt water as would pickle
Leviathan, and sighed enough to set up
Another wind;—

ORLANDO
Claudio, I pray thee, leave me;
I relish not this mockery.

CLAUDIO
Good sir, attend
To my experience. You've no stock as yet
To set up lover: get yourself a pistol
Without a touch-hole, or at least remember,
If it be whole, to load it with wet powder;
I've known a popgun, well applied, or even
The flying of a cork, give reputation
To courage and despair. A gross of garters,
Warranted rotten, will be found convenient.

ORLANDO
Now you are troublesome.

CLAUDIO
One precept more;
Purge and drink watergruel, lanthorn jaws
Are interesting; fat men can't write sonnets,
And indigestion turns true love to bile.

ORLANDO
'Tis best to part. If you desire to serve me,
Persuade the boy to sacrifice his passion;
I'll lead him to Olivia, they were wont
In childhood to be playmates, and some love
May lie beneath the ashes of that friendship,
That needs her breath alone to burst and blaze.

[Exeunt.

SCENE III

A Prison

Enter **GUARDS** leading **LORD ERNEST** in chains.

LORD ERNEST

I pray you do not pity me. I feel
A kind of joy to meet Calamity,
My old, old friend again. Go, tell your lord,
I give him thanks for these his iron bounties.
How now? I thought you led me to a prison,
A dismal antichamber of the tomb,
Where creatures dwell, whose ghosts but half inhabit
Their ruinous flesh-houses; here is air
As fresh as that the bird of morning sings in,
And shade that scarce is dusk, but just enough
To please the meek and twilight-loving eye
Of lone Religion. 'Tis an hermitage
Where I may sit and tell my o'erpassed years,
And fit myself for dying. My old heart
Holds not enough of gratitude to pay
This noble kindness, that in guise of cruelty
Compels me to my good.

GUARD

I am most glad
That you endure thus cheerfully; remember
Your son's one word will give you liberty.

LORD ERNEST

I know he would not do me so much wrong.
You think, because I'm white with age, I mourn
Such hardships. See, my hand's as firm and steady
As when I broke my first spear in the wars;
Alas! I am so glad, I cannot smile.

GUARD

We sorrow thus to leave thee.

LORD ERNEST

Sorrow! man,
It is a woman's game: I cannot play it.
Away; your whining but provokes my spleen.

[As the **GUARDS** are retiring he bursts into a harsh laugh: when they have left the stage he stops short.

They're gone and cannot hear me. Now, then, now,
Eyes weep away my life, heart, if thou hast
A pulse to strain, break, break, oh break!

[Enter **HESPERUS**.

My son,
Come here, I'll tell thee all they've done to me,
How they have scoffed and spurned me, thrown me here
In wretched loneliness

HESPERUS
Alas! my father.

LORD ERNEST
Oh set me free, I cannot bear this air.
If thou dost recollect those fearful hours,
When I kept watch beside my precious boy,
And saw the day but on his pale, dear face;
If thou didst think me, in my gentlest moods,
Patient and mild, and even somewhat kind;
Oh give me back the pity that I lent,
Pretend at least to love and comfort me.

HESPERUS
Speak not so harshly; I'm not rich enough
To pay one quarter of the dues of love,
Yet something I would do. Show me the way,
I will revenge thee well.

LORD ERNEST
But, whilst thou'rt gone,
The dread diseases of the place will come
And kill me wretchedly. No, I'll be free.

HESPERUS
Aye, that thou shalt. I'll do; what will I not?
I'll get together all the world's true hearts,
And if they're few, there's spirit in my breast
Enough to animate a thousand dead.

LORD ERNEST
My son
We need not this; a word of thine will serve.

HESPERUS
Were it my soul's last sigh I'd give it thee.

LORD ERNEST
Marry.

HESPERUS
I—cannot.

LORD ERNEST
But thou dost not know
Thy best-loved woos thee. Oft I've stood unseen,
In some of those sweet evenings you remember,
Watching your innocent and beauteous play,
(More innocent because you thought it secret,
More beautiful because so innocent;)
Oh! then I knew how blessed a thing I was
To have a son so worthy of Olivia.

HESPERUS
Olivia!

LORD ERNEST
Blush not, though I name your mistress;
You soon shall wed her.

HESPERUS
I will wed the plague.
I would not grudge my life, for that's a thing,
A misery, thou gavest me: but to wed
Olivia; there's damnation in the thought.

LORD ERNEST
Come, speak to him, my chains, for ye've a voice
To conquer every heart that's not your kin?
Oh! that ye were my son, for then at least
He would be with me. How I loved him once!
Aye, when I thought him good; but now—Nay, still
He must be good, and I, I have been harsh,
I feel, I have not prized him at his worth:
And yet I think, if Hesperus had erred,
I could have pardoned him, indeed I could.

HESPERUS
We'll live together.

LORD ERNEST
No, for I shall die;
But that's no matter.

HESPERUS
Bring the priest, the bride.
Quick, quick. These fetters have infected him
With slavery's sickness. Yet there is a secret,
'Twixt heaven and me, forbids it. Tell me, father;
Were it not best for both to die at once?

LORD ERNEST
Die! thou hast spoke a word, that makes my heart
Grow sick and wither; thou hast palsied me
To death. Live thou to wed some worthier maid;
Know that thy father chose this sad seclusion;
(Ye rebel lips, why do you call it sad?)
Should I die soon, think not that sorrow caused it,
But, if you recollect my name, bestow it
Upon your best-loved child, and when you give him
His Grandsire's blessing, add not that he perished
A wretched prisoner.

HESPERUS
Stop, or I am made
I know not what,—perhaps a villain. Curse me,
Oh if you love me, curse.

LORD ERNEST
Aye, thou shalt hear
A father's curse; if fate hath put a moment
Of pain into thy life; a sigh, a word,
A dream of woe; be it transferred to mine;
And for thy days; oh! never may a thought
Of others' sorrow, even of old Ernest's,
Darken their calm, uninterrupted bliss;
And be thy end—oh! any thing but mine.

HESPERUS
Guilt, thou art sanctified in such a cause;
Guards;

[They enter.

I am ready. Let me say't so low,
So quickly that it may escape the ear
Of watchful angels; I will do it all.

LORD ERNEST
There's nought to do; I've learned to love this solitude.
Farewell, my son. Nay, never heed the fetters;
We can make shift to embrace.

HESPERUS
Lead him to freedom,
And tell your lord I will not,—that's I will.

[Exeunt **LORD ERNEST** and **GUARDS**.

Here, fellow; put your hand upon my mouth
Till they are out of hearing. Leave me now.
No, stay; come near me, nearer yet. Now fix
The close attention of your eyes on mine.

GUARD
My lord!

HESPERUS
See'st thou not death in them?

GUARD
Forbid it, fate.

HESPERUS
Away! ill-omened hound;
I'll be a ghost and play about the graves,
For ghosts can never wed.

[Exit **GUARD**.

There, there they go; my hopes, my youthful hopes,
Like ingrate flatterers. What have I to do
With life? Ye sickly stars, that look with pity
On this cursed head, be kind and tell the lightning
To scathe me to a cinder; or if that
Be too much blessing for a child of sin,
But strike me mad, I do not ask for more.
Come from your icy caves, ye howling winds,
Clad in your gloomy panoply of clouds,
And call into your cars, as ye pass o'er
The distant quarters of this tortured world,
Every disease of every clime,
Here shall they banquet on a willing victim;
Or with one general ague shake the earth,
The pillars of the sky dissolve and burst,
And let the ebon-tiled roof of night
Come tumbling in upon the doomed world:—
Deaf are they still? then death is all a fable,
A pious lie to make man lick his chains
And look for freedom's dawning through his grate.
Why are we tied unto this wheeling globe,
Still to be racked while traitorous Hope stands by,
And heals the wounds that they may gape again?
Aye to this end the earth is made a ball,
Else crawling to the brink despair would plunge
Into the infinite eternal air,
And leave its sorrows and its sins behind.

Since death will not, come sleep, thou kindred power,
Lock up my senses with thy leaden key,
And darken every crevice that admits
Light, life, and misery, if thou canst, for ever.

[Exit.

A Chamber in Orlando's Palace

Enter **ORLANDO** to his **BOY** asleep.

ORLANDO
Boy! he is asleep;
Oh innocence, how fairly dost thou head
This pure, first page of man. Peace to thy slumbers;
Sleep, for thy dreams are 'midst the seraphs' harps,
Thy thoughts beneath the wings of holiness,
Thine eyes in Paradise.
The day may come, (if haply gentle death
Say not amen to thy short prayer of being,
And lap thee in the bosom of the blest;)
I weep to think on, when the guilty world
Shall, like a friend, be waiting at thy couch,
And call thee up on ev'ry dawn of crime.

BOY [awaking]
Dear master, didst thou call? I will not be
A second time so slothful.

ORLANDO
Sleep, my boy,
Thy task is light and joyous, to be good.

BOY
Oh! if I must be good, then give me money,
I pray thee, give me some, and you shall find
I'll buy up every tear, and make them scarcer
Than diamonds.

ORLANDO
Beautiful pity, thou shalt have enough;
But you must give me your last song.

BOY

Nay, sir;
You're wont to say my rhymes are fit for girls,
And lovesick ideots; I have none you praise
Full of the heat of battle and the chase.

ORLANDO

Sing what you will, I'll like it.

Song

A ho! A ho!
Love's horn doth blow,
And he will out a-hawking go.
His shafts are light as beauty's sighs,
And bright as midnight's brightest eyes,
And round his starry way
The swan-winged horses of the skies,
With summer's music in their manes,
Curve their fair necks to zephyr's reins,
And urge their graceful play.

A ho! A ho!
Love's horn doth blow,
And he will out a-hawking go.
The sparrows flutter round his wrist,
The feathery thieves that Venus kissed
And taught their morning song,
The linnets seek the airy list,
And swallows too, small pets of Spring,
Beat back the gale with swifter wing,
And dart and wheel along.

A ho! A ho!
Love's horn doth blow,
And he will out a-hawking go.
Now woe to every gnat that skips
To filch the fruit of ladies' lips,
His felon blood is shed;
And woe to flies, whose airy ships
On beauty cast their anchoring bite,
And bandit wasp, that naughty wight,
Whose sting is slaughter-red.

ORLANDO

Who is thy poet, boy?

BOY

I must not tell.

ORLANDO
Then I will chide thee for him. Who first drew
Love as a blindfold imp, an earthen dwarf,
And armed him with blunt darts? His soul was kin
To the rough wind that dwells in the icy north,
The dead, cold pedant, who thus dared confine
The universe's soul, for that is Love.
'Tis he that acts the nightingale, the thrush,
And all the living musics, he it is
That gives the lute, the harp, and tabor speech,
That flutters on melodious wings and strikes
The mute and viewless lyres of sunny strings
Borne by the minstrel gales, mimicking vainly
The timid voice, that sent him to my breast,
That voice the wind hath treasured and doth use
When he bids roses open and be sweet.

BOY
Now I could guess.

ORLANDO
What, little curious one?

BOY
The riddle of Orlando's feelings. Come,
You must not frown. I know the lawn, the cot,
Aye, and the leaf-veiled lattice.

ORLANDO
I shall task
Your busy watchfulness. Bear you this paper,
I would not trust it to a doubtful hand.

BOY
Unto the wood-nymph? You may think the road
Already footed.

ORLANDO
Go, and prosper then.

[Exeunt.

SCENE II

LENORA and **FLORIBEL**.

FLORIBEL
My mother, you're too kind, you ought to check
These wayward humours. Oh, I know too well
I'm a poor, foolish, discontented child;
My heart doth sink when Hesperus is gone,
And leaves me nought but fears. Forgive me then,
If I have vexed you.

LENORA
Dear and gentle soul,
You ne'er offended me, but when you said
You had offended. When I look on thee,
If there's a thought that moistens in my eye,
Fear, that thy husband cannot match such goodness,
Is looking out there.

FLORIBEL
Fears of Hesperus!
That's not my mother's thought, cast it away:
He is the glass of all good qualities,
And what's a little virtue in all others
Looks into him and sees itself a giant;
He is a nosegay of the sweets of man,
A dictionary of superlatives;
He walks about, a music among discords,
A star in night, a prayer 'midst madmen's curses;
And if mankind, as I do think, were made
To bear the fruit of him, and him alone,
It was a glorious destiny.

LENORA
He is a goodly man, and yet they say
Strange passions sleep within him. There's Orlando,
A gentle suitor; Floribel, he loved you,
He had no father, I have often wished
What it's too late to tell you.

FLORIBEL
Mother, your Orlando
Is a good gentleman, I wish him well,
But to my husband—We'll not talk of him.
Yet you shall see I can be cool sometimes,
When Hesperus deserves it, as he does
Even now for his delay.

LENORA
He's here: I'll leave you,
You shall not quarrel with him for my pleasure.

[Enter **HESPERUS**.

HESPERUS
Good morrow, Floribel.

FLORIBEL
Fair noon to Hesperus; I knew a youth,
In days of yore, would quarrel with the lark,
If with its joyous matins it foreran
His early pipe beneath his mistress' window;
Those days are passed; alas! for gallantry.

HESPERUS
Floribel!

FLORIBEL
Sir, d'ye know the gentleman?
Give him my benison and bid him sleep
Another hour, there's one that does not miss him.

HESPERUS
Lady, I came to talk of other things,
To tell you all my secrets: must I wait
Until it fits your humour?

FLORIBEL
As you please:
(The worst of three bad suitors, and his name
Began with an H.)

HESPERUS
Good morrow then, again.

FLORIBEL
Heaven help you, sir,
And so adieu.

HESPERUS
Madam, you spoke; you said it, Floribel:
I never thought mine ears a curse before.
Did I not love thee? Say, have I not been
The kindest?

FLORIBEL

Yes indeed thou hast been. Now
A month is over. What would I not give
For those four sevens of days? But I have lived them,
And that's a bliss. You speak as if I'd lost
The little love you gave your poor one then.

HESPERUS

And you as if you cared not for the loss.
Oh Floribel, you'll make me curse the chance
That fashioned this sad clay and made it man;
It had been happier as the senseless tree
That canopies your sleep. But Hesperus,
He's but the burthen of a scornful song
Of coquetry; beware, that song may end
In a death-groan.

FLORIBEL [sings]

The knight he left the maid,
That knight of fickleness,
Her's was the blame, he said,
And his the deep distress.

If you are weary of poor Floribel,
Pray be not troubled; she can do without thee.
Oh Hesperus, come hither, I must weep;
Say you will love me still, and I'll believe it,
When I forget my folly.

HESPERUS

Dear, I do;
By the bright fountains of those tears I do.

FLORIBEL

You don't despise me much? May I look up
And meet no frown?

HESPERUS

Try to look through my breast,
And see my truth. But, oh! my Floribel,
Take heed how thou dost look unkindly on me;
For grey-beards have been kneeling, and with prayers
Trying to pluck thee from my bosom; fairness,
And innocence, and duty league against thee.
Then do't not, sweet, again; for sometimes strange
And horrid thoughts bring whispers to my soul:
They shall not harm thee, girl. I meant indeed,
Hard hearted as I was, to have disclosed

A tale of terror; but I'll back again:
Why, let the old man die.

FLORIBEL
Oh no, no, no;
We will let no one die, but cherish them
With love like ours, and they will soon be well:
Stay and I'll tell you how to save him.

HESPERUS
Thou!
Excellent loveliness,
Thou save him! But I must be gone, or else
Those looks will lure a secret from my breast,
That threatens both. I'll home and think of something.
Meet me to-morrow in the sweet-briar thicket,
When twilight fades to evening. I'm in haste.

[Exit.

FLORIBEL
My better thoughts go with thee. It is true
He hath too much of human passion in him,
But I will hold him dear, and, if again
My wicked senses grow so cruel quick
As to suspect his kindness, I'll be sure
My eyes have got false sight, MY ears false hearing,
And my whole mind's become a rebel traitress.

Enter **ORLANDO's BOY**.

BOY
These for fair Floribel; you are the one
I hear my master talk of, surely, lady;
And yet his words are feeble shadowers
Of such pure beauty. Please you read his thoughts.

FLORIBEL
You hold a courtly language for such years;
But be you 'ware of compliment akin
To falsehood.
[Reads]
From the sad-souled Orlando.
Fie sir; your gifts are dangerous. Look you here,
As I disperse the wicked syllables
Met in this little parliament of words,
And give them to the light and careless winds,
So do I bid him tear the thoughts of me

Out of his breast, and hold me as a thing
Further from him than misery.

BOY
It is ungently done,—nay, I must say so,—
To hurt the generous blossoms of his love;
I am sorry that a hand so beautiful
Can be so fell.

FLORIBEL
Boy, thou dost not know
The fears that urge me. Had my Hesperus
Seen these or thee, I know not what of ill
Must have befallen us.

BOY
Lady, you must not weep;
I have a ballad which my master hears
In his sad moods; it has the art to raise
A dimple on the cheek of moody care.
I'll sing it you.

FLORIBEL
Young one, I almost love thee.

[Kisses him.

[Enter **HESPERUS**.

HESPERUS
Why Floribel,—Girl! Painted fickleness!
Madam, I'm rude; but Hesperus did not think
He could intrude on—what was Floribel.

FLORIBEL
Nor doth he ever.

HESPERUS
If he does not now,
Be sure he won't again. Oh girl, girl, girl,
Thou'st killed my heart: I thought thee once, good fool,
I will not tell thee what, thou'lt laugh at me.

FLORIBEL
By heaven!

HESPERUS
Don't name it: do not be forsworn.

But why should I regard thy words or oaths?

FLORIBEL
Hesperus, Hesperus!

HESPERUS
Nay, I should be sorry
To cheat the longing boy; he fills thine arms
Excellent well, believe it. Urchin, seek me
When that mis-featured butter-print of thine
Is bearded; I will trim thee with a sword.

FLORIBEL
Hesperus, thou art mad.

HESPERUS
Better be mad than treacherous. Aye, 'twas well
To tear the letters; there might be a husband;
No, he shall be no more.

FLORIBEL
But listen to me,
These lips that thou hast kissed,—

HESPERUS
I, and a thousand,
Men, boys, and monsters.

FLORIBEL
And these arms thou callest
Beloved and fair—

HESPERUS
And fickle and adulterous.
Enough of woman: boy, your paramour
Is troublesome, sirrah, milk-blooded imp,
Raise her; she loves your silken limbs; I give you
All that is mine of her.

FLORIBEL
Oh! save me, dearest.

HESPERUS
She speaks to you, sir. I beseech you both,
Go on; don't heed me: oh, I joy to see
Your love-tricks.

FLORIBEL

By the solemn spousal tie,
I charge you, hear me.

HESPERUS
Lady, I will tell you,
Though it is needless, what I meant to say,
And leave you then for ever. You remember
A loving dupe you entertained some while,
One Hesperus, you must; oh! that you ever
Forgot him. Well, I Will be brief. He gave you,
And bade you keep it as you would his love,
A little bird, a sweet red-bosomed creature,
To toy with in his absence: (then he knew not
You had another playmate for your chamber.)
This bird, it was a creature that I loved,
Yet it did not deceive me; I have thought
There was a spirit in it—never mind;
I dreamed I spoke to one, who valued me
And my poor feelings. Unto you I gave it,
And you have lost it; in my way I passed
Its silent wicker house. Now I have spoken,
Perhaps was tedious: but I'm still so foolish,
That I will say, good bye.

FLORIBEL
Oh stay, my love.

HESPERUS
He will, the lovely cub.

FLORIBEL
Thee, thee I mean.

HESPERUS
I am no lover, I. Madam, we're strangers;
And yet I knew some while ago a form
Like thine, as fair, as delicate. Oh heaven!
To think of it. But she was innocent,
Innocent, innocent.

FLORIBEL
The angels know
I am as spotless.

HESPERUS
Go to them; I'm not one;
Perhaps this pap-faced chit may be. Nay, girl,
Wet not thy cheeks: I've seen a player weep.

I will not go, for if I do, the flock
Of her warm suitors will be toying here;
Yet I'll not stay; for she will melt and pray
Till I'm a fool again. Strain not your lungs
With laughter when I'm gone. Oh woman, woman.

[Exit.

FLORIBEL
Poor boy, thou hast undone me: lead me in.

[Exeunt.

SCENE III

An Apartment in Orlando's Palace

Enter **HESPERUS**.

HESPERUS
Oh thou sad self, thou wretched half of Hesperus,
Thou'rt lost indeed, there's nought of life about thee,
But the one thought, that thou hast saved a father.
Now I do think that if I meet a goodness
In woman's shape, a fair one I'd not ask,
But something that would soothe and comfort me,
I could almost love her.

[Enter **ORLANDO** and **OLIVIA**.

ORLANDO
My brother Hesperus, our poor home is honoured
By thy loved father's presence and thine own.
Here is a living welcome, prithee know her;
Olivia.

HESPERUS
Blessedness, you should have said.
A music waits upon her every step,
That my heart leaps to.

OLIVIA
Courtly, sir, and kind.

HESPERUS
And fond I would have made it. Oh fair lady,

A smile of thine will give me health again.

ORLANDO
Sister, thou needst no witness to these blushes.
School her, sir, in the arts of compliment,
You'll find her an apt learner.

[Exit.

OLIVIA
Had I a right to pray to you, I would.

HESPERUS
Pray, lady? Didst thou ever see the goddess
Step from her dignity of stone, or leave
The hallowed picture in its tinted stole,
And crouch unto her suppliant? Oh no;
If there is aught so poor a thing as I
Can please you with, command it and you bless me.

OLIVIA
Try, I beseech thee, try not to detest,
Not utterly to detest a silly girl,
Whose only merit is that she'd be thine.

HESPERUS
Hate thee, thou virtue?

OLIVIA
Well, if it must be,
Play the deceiver for a little while;
Don't tell me so.

HESPERUS
By Truth's white name I'll tell thee,
Olivia, there was once an idle thought
That aped affection in my heart; nay, nay,
Not in my heart; it was a dream or so;
A dream within a dream; a pale, dim warmth;
But thou hast dawned like summer on my soul,
Or like a new existence.

OLIVIA
'Twere delightful,
If credible; but you are all too gallant.

HESPERUS
I knew it must be so: you'll not believe me,

But doubt and say 'tis sudden. Do not minute
The movements of the soul, for some there are,
Of pinion unimpeded, thrice word-swift,
Outsoar the sluggish flesh; and these, Olivia,
Anticipating their death-given powers, can grasp
A century of feeling and of thought;
Outlive the old world's age, and be at once
In the present, past, and future; while the body
Lives half a pulse's stroke. To see and love thee
Was but one soul's step.

OLIVIA
Then thou canst endure me;
Thou dost not hate the forward maid? My prayer
Through many a year has been for that one word;
And I have kept the precious thought of thee,
Hidden almost from myself. But I'll not speak,
For I have told too much, too childishly.

HESPERUS
Dear, I could weep, but that my brain is dry,
To think upon thee. Me—'Twere well to court
The yellow pestilence, or woo the lightning
Unto thy bosom; but to hold me dear—
It is a crime of hell; forget you thought it.

OLIVIA
'Tis sweeter than a virtue, I must love thee.

HESPERUS
And love me truly?

OLIVIA
Heaven grant me life
To prove it.

HESPERUS
Then thou shalt be mine own; but not till death:
We'll let this life burn out, no matter how;
Though every sand be moistened with our tears,
And every day be rain-wet in our eyes;
Though thou shouldst wed some hateful avarice,
And I grow hoary with a daubed deceit,
A smiling treachery in woman's form,
Sad to the soul, heart-cankered and forlorn;
No matter, all no matter.
Though madness rule our thoughts, despair our hearts,
And misery live with us, and misery talk,

Our guest all day, our bed-fellow all night;
No matter, all no matter.
For when our souls are born then will we wed;
Our dust shall mix and grow into one stalk,
Our breaths shall make one perfume in one bud,
Our blushes meet each other in a rose,
Our sweeter voices swell some sky-bird's throat
With the same warbling, dwell in some soft pipe,
Or bubble up along some sainted spring's
Musical course, and in the mountain trees
Slumber our deeper tones, by tempests waked:
We will be music, spring, and all fair things,
The while our spirits make a sweeter union
Than melody and perfume in the air.
Wait then, if thou dost love me.

OLIVIA
Be it so;
You'll let me pray for death, if it will bring
Such joys as these? Though once I thought to live
A happy bride; but I must learn new feelings.

HESPERUS
New feelings! Aye to watch the lagging clock,
And bless each moment as it parts from thee,
To court the blighting grasp of tardy age,
And search thy forehead for a silver tress
As for a most prized jewel.

OLIVIA
I cannot think
Of that cold bed diseases make for us,
That earthy sleep; oh! 'tis a dreadful thing.

HESPERUS
The very air,
I thank it, (the same wild and busy air,
That numbers every syllable I speak,
In the same instant my lips shape its sound,
With the first lisps of him, who died before
The world began its story;) steals away
A little from my being;
And at each slightest tremour of a leaf
My hearse moves one step nearer. Joy, my love!
We're nearer to our bridal sheets of lead
Than when your brother left us here just now,
By twenty minutes talk.

OLIVIA

It is not good
Thus to spurn life, the precious gift of heaven,
And watch the coming light of dissolution
With such a desperate hope. Can we not love
In secret, and be happy in our thoughts,
Till in devotion's train, th' appointed hour
Lead us, with solemnly rejoicing hearts,
Unto our blessed end?

HESPERUS

End! thou sayest.
And do those cherries ripen for the worms,
Those blue enchantments beam to light the tomb?
Was that articulate harmony, (Love uses
Because he seems both Love and Innocence
When he sings to it,) that summer of sweet breath,
Created but to perish and so make
The deads' home loveliest?

OLIVIA

But what's to live without my Hesperus?
A life of dying. 'Tis to die each moment
In every several sense. To look despair,
Feel, taste, breathe, eat, be conscious of despair.
No, I'll be nothing rather.

HESPERUS

Nothing but mine!
Thou flower of love, I'll wear thee in my bosom;
With thee the wrath of man will be no wrath,
Conscience and agony will smile like pleasure,
And sad remembrance lose its gloomy self
In rapturous expectation.

OLIVIA

Let me look on thee;
Pray pardon me, mine eyes are very fools.

HESPERUS

Jewels of pity, azure stars of beauty
Which lost affection steers by; could I think
To dim your light with sorrow? Pardon me,
And I will serve you ever. Sweet, go in;
Somewhat I have to think on.

[Exit **OLIVIA**.

Floribel,
I would not have thee cross my path to night;
There is an indistinct dread purpose forming,
Something, whose depth of wickedness appears
Hideous, incalculable, but inevitable;
Now it draws nearer, and I do not shudder;
Avaunt! haunt me no more; I dread it not,
But almost—hence! I must not be alone.

[Exit

SCENE IV

A Tapestried Chamber in the Same

HESPERUS discovered in a disturbed slumber.

HESPERUS [starting from his couch]
Who speaks?
Who whispers there? A light! a light!
I'll search the room, something hath called me thrice,
With a low muttering voice of toadish hisses,
And thrice I slept again. But still it came
Nearer and nearer, plucked my mantle from me,
And made mine heart an ear, in which it poured
Its loathed enticing courtship. Ho! a light.

[Enter ATTENDANT with a torch.

Thou drowsy snail, thy footsteps are asleep,
Hold up the torch.

ATTENDANT
My lord, you are disturbed.
Have you seen aught?

HESPERUS
I lay upon my bed,
And something in the air, out-jetting night,
Converting feeling to intenser vision,
Featured its ghastly self upon my soul
Deeper than sight.

ATTENDANT
This is Delusion surely;
She's busy with men's thoughts at all night hours,

And to the waking subtle apprehension
The darkling chamber's still and sleepy air
Hath breath and motion oft.

HESPERUS
Lift up the hangings, mark the doors, the corners;
Seest nothing yet? No face of fiendlike mirth,
More frightful than the fixed and doggish grin
Of a dead madman?

ATTENDANT
Nought I see, my lord,
Save the long, varied crowd of warlike shapes
Set in the stitched picture.

HESPERUS
Heard ye then?
There was a sound, as though some marble tongue
Moved on its rusty hinge, syllabling harshly
The hoarse death-rattle into speech.

ATTENDANT
The wind is high, and through the silent rooms
Murmurs his burthen, to an heedless ear
Almost articulate.

HESPERUS
Thou sleepest, fool;
A voice has been at my bedside to-night,
Its breath is burning on my forehead still,
Still o'er my brain its accents, wildly sweet,
Hover and fall. Away and dream again:
I'll watch myself.

[He takes the torch and turns to the hangings.

[Exit **ATTENDANT**.

Aye, these are living colours,
Those cheeks have worn their youth these hundred years,
Those flowers are verdant in their worsted spring
And blooming still;
While she, whose needle limned so cunningly,
Sleeps and dreams not. It is a goodly state,
And there is one I wish had ta'en her bed
In the stone dormitory.
(Blindfold moth,
Thou shalt not burn thy life; there, I have saved thee;

If thou art grateful, mingle with the air
That feeds the lips of her I thought of once,
Choak her, moth, choak her. I could be content,
If she were safe in heaven.)
Yon stout dagger
Is fairly fashioned for a blade of stitches,
And shines, methinks, most grimly; well, thou art
An useful tool sometimes, thy tooth works quickly,
And, if thou gnawest a secret from the heart,
Thou tellest it not again: ha! the feigned steel
Doth blush and steam. There is a snuff of blood.

[Grasps his dagger convulsively.

Who placed this iron aspic in my hand?
Speak! who is at my ear?

[He turns, and addresses his shadow.

I know thee now,
I know the hideous laughter of thy face.
'Tis Malice' eldest imp, the heir of hell,
Red-handed Murther. Slow it whispers me,
Coaxingly with its serpent voice. Well sung,
Syren of Acheron!
I'll not look on thee;
Why does thy frantic weapon dig the air
With such most frightful vehemence? Back, back,
Tell the dark grave I will not give it food.
Back to thy home of night. What! playest thou still?
Then thus I banish thee. Out, treacherous'torch,
Sure thou wert kindled in infernal floods,
Or thy bright eye would blind at sights like this.

[Dashes the torch on the ground.

Tempt me no more; I tell thee, Floribel
Shall never bleed. I pray thee, guilty word,
Tempt me no more.

[Wraps himself in his mantle.

I'm deaf, my ears are safe,
I do not hear thee woo me to the deed;
Thou tellest to one without auricular sense
Olivia's beauties and that bad one's faults.
Oh! bring me thoughts of pity. Come, come, come,
Or I am lost.

Bad goblin, must I fly thee?

[Exit.

SCENE V

A Hall in the Same

LORD ERNEST, ORLANDO, CLAUDIO, OLIVIA.

LORD ERNEST
Saw ye my son?

OLIVIA
Some hours ago we parted,
And he was strange, though gentle, in his talk.

ORLANDO
I passed him in the garden, just at twilight,
He stood with eyes wide open, but their sense
Dreamed, in dumb parley with some fancied thing;
For his lips moved, and he did walk and gaze,
Now frown most mournfully, now smile most madly,
And weep, and laugh, groan deep and gnash his teeth,
And now stand still with such a countenance,
As does the marble sorrow o'er a tomb.
At last he tore his feet, as they were roots,
Up from the earth, and sighed like one o'ercome;
Then, with his fingers thrust upon his eyes
And dashed unclosed away, he seemed to snatch
Some loathly object out of them, and leapt
Into the thicket's gloom.

LORD ERNEST
Who saw him since?

CLAUDIO
In most distempered wildness he hath left
His chamber now.

LORD ERNEST
Go seek him, every one,
I do beseech you; 'tis a fearful period,
I know too truly. On his nurse's breast,
Some twenty years ago, he lay and mused
Upon her singing and bright merry lips;

A viewless bolt dropped on her, and she died
Most hideously; close in the infant's face
Looked all the horrors of her bursting eyes;
And, as the months bring round that black remembrance,
His brain unsettles, bloody thoughts oppress
And call him from his bed. Search all the darkness,
Each one a several way; dear daughter, in.

[Exeunt.

SCENE VI

A Suicide's Grave

ORLANDO and **CLAUDIO**.

CLAUDIO
There is a plague in this night's breath, Orlando,
The dews fall black and blistering from yon cloud
Anchored above us; dost thou mark how all
The smokes of heaven avoid it and crowd on
Far from its fatal darkness? Some men say
That the great king of evil sends his spirits
In such a winged car, to stir ill minds
Up to an act of death.

ORLANDO
We may not think so,
For there's a fascination in bad deeds,
Oft pondered o'er, that draws us to endure them,
And then commit. Beware of thine own soul:
'Tis but one devil ever tempts a man,
And his name's Self. Know'st thou these rankling hemlocks?

CLAUDIO
I've seen the ugsome reptiles battening on them,
While healthy creatures sicken at the sight.

ORLANDO
Five months ago they were an human heart,
Beating in Hugo's breast. A parricide
Here sleeps, self-slaughtered. 'Twas a thing of grace,
In his early infancy; I've known him oft
Outstep his pathway, that he might not crush
The least small reptile. But there is a time
When goodness sleeps; it came, and vice was grafted

On his young thoughts, and grew, and flourished there:
Envenomed passions clustered round that prop;
A double fruit they bore; a double fruit of death.

CLAUDIO
Enough, Orlando,
The imps of darkness listen, while we tell
A dead man's crimes. Even now I heard a stir,
As if the buried turned them in their shrouds
For mere unquiet. Home, it is the time
When the hoarse fowl, the carrier-bird of woe,
Brings fevers from the moon, and maddening dreams;
The hour's unholy, and who hath not sent
After the parted sun his orisons,
Falls 'neath the sway of evil.

[Exeunt.

[Enter **HESPERUS**.

HESPERUS
Hail, shrine of blood, in double shadows veiled,
Where the Tartarian blossoms shed their poison
And load the air with wicked impulses;
Hail, leafless shade, hallowed to sacrilege,
Altar of death! Where is thy deity?
With him I come to covenant, and thou,
Dark power, that sittest in the chair of night,
Searching the clouds for tempests with thy brand,
Proxy of Hades; list and be my witness,
And bid your phantoms all, (the while I speak
What, if they but repeat in sleeping ears,
Will strike the hearer dead, and mad his soul;)
Spread wide and black and thick their cloudy wings,
Lest the appalled sky do pale to-day.
Eternal people of the lower world,
Ye citizens of Hades' capitol,
That by the rivers of remorseful tears
Sit and despair for ever;
Ye negro brothers of the deadly winds,
Ye elder souls of night, ye mighty sins,
Sceptred damnations, how may man invoke
Your darkling glories? Teach my eager soul
Fit language for your ears. Ye that have power
O'er births and swoons and deaths, the soul's attendants,
(Wont to convey her from her human home
Beyond existence, to the past or future,
To lead her through the starry-blossomed meads,

Where the young hours of morning by the lark
With earthly airs are nourished, through the groves
Of silent gloom, beneath whose breathless shades
The thousand children of Calamity
Play murtherously with men's hearts:) Oh pause,
Your universal occupations leave,
Lay down awhile the infant miseries,
That, to the empty and untenanted clay,
Ye carry from the country of the unborn;
And grant the summoned soul one moment more
To linger on the threshold of its flesh;
For I would task you.
Bear this breath of mine,
This inner Hesperus away, and bring
Another guest to its deserted home;
The mind of him whose dust is on my feet,
And let his daring spirit inhabit there
But for a passing day.
'Tis here. A wind
Is rushing through my veins, and I become
As a running water.
I see a shadowy image of myself,
Yet not my perfect self, a brother self,
That steps into my bosom. Am I born
Newly, or newly dead? I'll think a little.
Have I e'er lived before, or thought or acted?
Why no; it was the morning doze of being,
I slept content with dreams; but now I wake
And find it noon, a time for stirring deeds.
Yes, this is life that trembles in my veins,
Yes, this is courage warms my heart's full tide:
Hesperus is a man, a demon-man,
And there's a thing he lives for, shall amaze
The emulous bad powers.
Lead me on,
Mysterious guide, companion wickedness;
Olivia calls me forward, and, to reach her,
What if we tread upon a world of hearts?
Come, ye ill blasts, ye killing visitants
Of sleeping men, wild creatures of the air,
We'll walk together; come, ye beauteous snakes,
Ye lovely fanged monsters of the woods,
We'll grovel in the dust and ye shall hiss
Your tunes of murder to me.

[An ignis fatuus rises.

Lo, she's here

To light our sports, the Hebe of the dead,
Alecto, 'mid her nest of living hair
Bearing a star of Tartarus. Lead on.

[Exit.

_*

ACT III

SCENE I

An Apartment in Orlando's Palace

HESPERUS seated. **ATTENDANTS**. Enter to them **CLAUDIO**.

CLAUDIO
The bridegroom's here?

ATTENDANT
Yonder he sits, my lord,
And since the morn's first hour, without the motion
Even of a nerve, as he were growing marble,
Has sat and watched: the sun blazed in at noon
With light enough to blind an eagle's ken;
He felt it not, although his eyeballs glared
Horribly bright: I spoke; he heard me not;
And, when I shook his arm, slept on in thought:
I pray you try him.

CLAUDIO
Sir, good Hesperus,
I wait at your desire; we are to end
Our match at tennis. Will you walk with me?

ATTENDANT
Your voice is weak as silence to his sense.

[Enter **ORLANDO**.

ORLANDO
My brother, you must join us at the banquet;
We wait your coming long; how's this?

ATTENDANT
My lord,
Like trance has held him since the dawn of day;
He has looked down upom yon wood since then,

Speechless and still.

[Enter **LORD ERNEST**.

LORD ERNEST
Now health and good be here,
For I have missed my son the livelong day.
Why, what an idle loiterer thou art;
By this, your vacant sight must ache with gazing
Upon that view. Arise; I'd have you with me,
To fix upon some posy for the ring
You wed your love with. Death! Some fearful change
Is here. Speak; speak and tell me if he lives.

ATTENDANT
He does, my lord, if breathing is to live,
But in all else is like the coffined dead;
Motion and speech he lacks.

LORD ERNEST
O heavens! Orlando,
Tell me 'tis false.

ORLANDO
I would 'twere in my power,
But it doth seem too true.

LORD ERNEST
Ride like the wind,
Fetch him the aid of medicine. See you not
Some vision has come to him in the night,
And stolen his eyes and ears and tongue away?

[Enter **OLIVIA**.

Oh, you are come in time to see him die;
Look, look, Olivia, look; he knows us not;
My son, if thou dost hear me, speak one word,
And I will bless thee.

ORLANDO
He is dumb indeed.

OLIVIA
Let me come near him. Dearest Hesperus,
If thou behold'st these poor unbeauteous cheeks,
Which first thy flattering kindness taught to blush;
Or if thou hearest a voice, that's only sweet

When it says Hesperus; oh gentle love,
Speak any thing, even that thou hatest Olivia,
And I will thank thee for't: or, if some horror
Has frozen up the fountain of thy words,
Give but a sign.

CLAUDIO
Lady, alas, 'tis vain.

OLIVIA [kneeling]
Nay, he shall speak, or I will never move,
But thus turn earth beseeching his dull hand,
And let the grass grow over me. I'll hold
A kind of converse with my raining eyes,
For if he sees not, nor doth hear, he'll know
The gentle feel of his Olivia's tears.

CLAUDIO
Sweet sir, look on her.

ORLANDO
Brother!

OLIVIA
Husband!

LORD ERNEST
Son!
Kind heaven, let him hear, though death should call him.

[Pause, a clock strikes.

HESPERUS
The hour is come.

[Exit.

SCENE II

A Room in Mordred's Cottage

FLORIBEL alone.

FLORIBEL
And must I wake again? Oh come to me,
Thou that with dew-cold fingers softly closest

The wearied eye; thou sweet, thou gentle power,
Soother of woe, sole friend of the oppressed,
I long to lay me on thy peaceful breast.
But once I saw thee, beautiful as moonlight,
Upon a baby's lips, and thou didst kiss them,
Lingering and oft,
(As a wild bee doth kiss a rifled flower,
And clips its waist, and drops a little tear,
Remorsefully enamoured of his prey;)
Come so to me, sweet death, and I will wreath thee
An amorous chaplet for thy paly brows;
And, on an odoured bank of wan white buds,
In thy fair arms
I'll lie, and taste thy cool delicious breath,
And sleep, and sleep, and sleep.

[Enter **LENORA**.

O here, good mother,
We'll talk together.

LENORA
What; of Hesperus?
Methinks he has grown cold.

FLORIBEL
Oh no; he is
More full of courtship than he ever was;
Don't think him cold, dear mother, or I may:
I'm sure he loves me still; I'll go to him,
'Tis nigh the appointed hour.

LENORA
My child, it is a chill and gloomy evening,
So go not out. Thy Hesperus will come,
And thou wilt live on every word of his
Till thine eyes sparkle. What means this despondence?

FLORIBEL
Dear mother, I will strive to be at ease,
If you desire; but melancholy thoughts
Are poor dissemblers. How I wish we owned
The wealth we've lost.

LENORA
Why girl, I never heard
One such regret escape your lips before;
Has not your Hesperus enough?

FLORIBEL

Too much;
If he were even poorer than ourselves,
I'd almost love him better. For, methinks,
It seemed a covetous spirit urged me on,
Craving to be received his bride. I hope
He did not think so; if he does, I'll tell him
I will not share his wealth, but dwell with you.
O that he'd come! How each dull moment drags
Its lazy wing along when he is absent.
When was he here?

LENORA

Last night.

FLORIBEL

Last night? Now pr'ythee
Don't jeer me so, I'm sure, not many days;
But all is night when he's not here to light me,
So let it be last night; although that night
Had days for hours, yet in Love's book and mine
'Tis but an empty cypher, a black round.
Oh, I've not lived, I've not been Floribel
Since the last mellow echo of his voice
Lent the air music; is't not a sweet voice?
What can you liken to it?

LENORA

Pan's honeycomb
Of many vocal cells.

FLORIBEL

How dull you are;
There's nought beneath the thunder-choir so grand;
The wood-birds and the waterfalls but mock him.
He said, dear mother, I should be his countess;
To-day he'd come to fetch me, but with day
I've laid my expectation in its grave.
Dost think he will deceive me? Silly girl,
Querulous ingrate, why do I torment me?
Sweet mother, comfort.

LENORA

Be you sure he'll come
With his whole princely train of friends and kindred,
And he will lift thee to his gorgeous car,
And place thee at his side, a happy wife.

FLORIBEL
Fie! you cajole me, like a sulky child,
With gilded cars; but oh! I wish 'twere here.
How gloomily the clouds look, and the wind
Rattles among the brown leaves dolefully;
He will be very chill, heap up the fire.
Hush! hark! What's that?

LENORA
Only your dear father
Heavily breathing in his sleep; he'll wake
With his sad smile upon his patient face,
Looking so dear in sickness.

FLORIBEL
But 'twill cure him,
When he knows all and sees my bridegroom with me,
I know it will: and there's the horse's step,
I'll just run out, it is not cold at all.—

LENORA
Go, my love,
But you must come to ask your father's blessing,
And bring your Hesperus with you.

FLORIBEL
That I will.

[Exeunt.

SCENE III

A Wood

Enter **HUBERT** and a **HUNTSMAN**.

HUBERT
No answer to our shouts but mocking echo?
Where are our fellow huntsmen? Why, they vanished
Like mist before the sun, and left us here
Lost in the briary mazes.

HUNTSMAN
Shame on the rogues
For this their treatment. But look upwards, Hubert,

See what a mighty storm hangs right above us.

HUBERT
The day is in its shroud while yet an infant;
And Night with giant strides stalks o'er the world,
Like a swart Cyclops, on its hideous front
One round, red, thunder-swollen eye ablaze.

HUNTSMAN
Now mercy save the peril-stricken man,
Who 'mongst his shattered canvas sits aghast
On the last sinking plank alone, and sees
The congregated monsters of the deep
For his dead messmates warring all, save one
That leers upon him with a ravenous gaze,
And whets its iron tusks just at his feet:
Yet little heeds his wide and tearless eye
That, or the thunder of the mountain flood
Which Destiny commissions with his doom;
Where the wild waters rush against the sky,
Far o'er the desolate plain, his star of hope
In mockery gleams, while Death is at his side.

[Lightning.

HUBERT
That flash hath rent the heavens; this way for shelter.

HUNTSMAN
Some steps above there stands a noble oak,
That from the sun roofs ever-during night
With its thickwoven firmament of leaves:
Thither betake we.

[Exeunt.

[Enter **FLORIBEL**.

FLORIBEL
Hence did I seem to hear a human voice,
Yet there is nought, save a low moaning sound,
As if the spirits of the earth and air
Were holding sad and ominous discourse.
And much I fear me I have lost my path;
Oh how these brambles tear; here 'twixt the willows;
Ha! something stirs; my silly prattling nurse
Says that fierce shaggy wolves inhabit here,
And 'tis in sooth a dread and lonely place;

There, there again; a rustling in the leaves.

[Enter **HESPERUS**.

'Tis he at last; why dost thou turn away
And lock thy bosom from my first embrace?
I am so tired and frightened; but thou'rt here;
I knew thou wouldst be faithful to thy promise,
And claim me openly. Speak, let me hear thy voice,
Tell me the joyful news.

HESPERUS
Aye, I am come
In all my solemn pomp; Darkness and Fear,
And the great Tempest in his midnight car,
The sword of lightning girt across his thigh,
And the whole dæmon brood of night, blind Fog
And withering Blight, all these are my retainers;
How: not one smile for all this bravery?
What think you of my minstrels, the hoarse winds,
Thunder, and tuneful Discord? Hark, they play.
Well piped, methinks; somewhat too rough, perhaps.

FLORIBEL
I know you practise on my silliness,
Else I might well be scared. But leave this mirth,
Or I must weep.

HESPERUS
'Twill serve to fill the goblets
For our carousal; but we loiter here,
The bridemaids are without; well-picked thou'lt say,
Wan ghosts of woe-begone, self-slaughtered damsels
In their best winding sheets; start not, I bid them wipe
Their gory bosoms; they'll look wondrous comely;
Our link-boy, Will o' the Wisp, is waiting too
To light us to our grave—bridal I mean.

FLORIBEL
Ha! how my veins are chilled—why, Hesperus!

HESPERUS
What hero of thy dreams art calling, girl?
Look in my face—Is't mortal? Dost thou think
The voice that calls thee is not of a mouth
Long choaked with dust? What, though I have assumed
This garb of flesh, and with it the affections,
The thoughts of weakness and mortality?

'Twas but for thee; and now thou art my bride;
Lift up thine eyes and smile—the bride of Death.

FLORIBEL

Hold, hold. My thoughts are wildered. Is my fancy
The churlish framer of these fearful words,
Or do I live indeed to such a fate?
Oh! no, I recollect; I have not waked
Since Hesperus left me in the twilight bower.

HESPERUS

Come, we'll to our chamber,
The cypress shade hangs o'er our stony couch,
A goodly canopy; be mad and merry;
There'll be a jovial feast among the worms.
Fiends, strew your fiercest fire about my heart,
[aside.
Or she will melt it.

FLORIBEL

Oh, that look of fury!
What's this about my eyes? ah! deadly night,
No light, no hope, no help.

HESPERUS

What! Darest thou tremble
Under thy husband's arm, darest think of fear?
Dost dread me, me?

FLORIBEL

I know not what to dread,
Nor what to hope; all's horrible and doubtful;
And coldness creeps—

HESPERUS

She swoons, poor girl, she swoons.
And, treacherous dæmons, ye've allowed a drop
To linger in my eyes. Out, out for ever.
I'm fierce again. Now shall I slay the victim
As she lies senseless? ah! she wakes; cheer up,
'Twas but a jest.

FLORIBEL

A dread and cruel one;
But I'll forgive you, if you will be kind;
And yet 'twas frightful.

HESPERUS

Why, 'twere most unseemly
For one marked for the grave to laugh too loud.

FLORIBEL
Alas! he raves again. Sweetest, what mean you
By these strange words?

HESPERUS
What mean I? Death and murder,
Darkness and misery. To thy prayers and shrift;
Earth gives thee back; thy God hath sent me for thee;
Repent and die.

FLORIBEL
Oh, if thou willest it, love,
If thou but speak it with thy natural voice,
And smile upon me; I'll not think it pain,
But cheerfully I'll seek me out a grave,
And sleep as sweetly as on Hesperus' breast.
He will not smile, he will not listen to me.
Why dost thou thrust thy fingers in thy bosom?
Oh search it, search it; see if there remain
One little remnant of thy former love,
To dry my tears with.

HESPERUS
Well, speak on; and then,
When thou hast done thy tale, I will but kill thee.
Come tell me all my vows, how they are broken,
Say that my love was feigned, and black deceit;
Pour out thy bitterest, till untamed wrath
Melt all his chains off with his fiery breath,
And rush a-hungering out.

FLORIBEL
Oh piteous heavens!
I see it now, some wild and poisonous creature
Hath wounded him, and with contagious fang
Planted this fury in his veins. He hides
The mangled fingers; dearest, trust them to me,
I'll suck the madness out of every pore,
So as I drink it boiling from thy wound
Death will be pleasant. Let me have the hand,
And I will treat it like another heart.

HESPERUS
Here 'tis then;

[Stabs her.

Shall I thrust deeper yet?

FLORIBEL
Quite through my soul,—
That all my senses, deadened at the blow,
May never know the giver. Oh, my love,
Some spirit in thy sleep hath stolen thy body
And filled it to the brim with cruelty.
Farewell! and may no busy deathful tongue
Whisper this horror in thy waking ears,
Lest some dread desperate sorrow urge thy soul
To deeds of wickedness. Whose kiss is that?
His lips are ice. Oh my loved Hesperus,
Help!

[Dies.

HESPERUS
What a shriek was that; it flew to heaven,
And hymning angels took it for their own.
Dead art thou, Floribel; fair, painted earth,
And no warm breath shall ever more disport
Between those rubious lips: no, they have quaffed
Life to the dregs, and found death at the bottom,
The sugar of the draught. All cold and still;
Her very tresses stiffen in the air.
Look, what a face: had our first mother worn
But half such beauty, when the serpent came,
His heart, all malice, would have turned to love.
No hand but this, which I do think was once
Cain, the arch-murtherer's, could have acted it.
And I must hide these sweets, not in my bosom;
In the foul earth. She shudders at my grasp;
Just so she laid her head across my bosom
When first—oh villain! which way lies the grave?

[Exit.

[Enter **HUBERT** and a **HUNTSMAN**.

HUBERT
It is a fearful and tempestuous time:
The concave firmament, the angel's bridge
O'er the world's day and night, is visibly
Bowed down and bent beneath its load of thunder;
And through the fiery fissures of the clouds

Glistens the warfare of armed elements,
Bellowing defiance in earth's stunned ear,
And setting midnight on the throne of day.

HUNTSMAN
The roar has ceased; the hush of intercalm
'Numbs with its leaden finger Echo's lips,
And angry spirits in mid havoc pause,
Premeditating ruin in their silence.

HUBERT
Hard by should stand a lone and tattered shed,
Where some tired woodsman may by chance be stretched,
Watching his scanty food among the coals;
There may we chafe our drenched and chilly limbs.

HUNTSMAN
The forest has more tenants than I knew:
Look underneath this branch; seest thou not yonder,
Amongst the brushwood and the briary weeds,
A man at work?

HUBERT
My life upon't some miser,
Who in the secret hour creeps to his hoard,
And, kneeling at the altar of his love,
Worships that yellow devil, gold.

HUNTSMAN
'Tis buried;
And now he stamps the sod down, that no light
May spy his mistress; with what a doleful look
He marks its grave, and backward walks away,
As if he left his all of sight behind.

HUBERT
Let us steal towards it; I would have a peep
Upon this hidden jewel.

[Exeunt.

[Enter **HESPERUS**.

HESPERUS
Shall I turn back and try to thrust my soul
In at her lips, and so re-animate
The beauteous casket while this body dies?
I cannot:—not the universe of breath

Could give those little lips their life again.
I've huddled her into the wormy earth,
And left the guilty dagger at her side.
Dead Innocence! and must unkindly thistles,
And rank thick hemlock, force their bristling roots
Into thy lovely breast? Fool! Is't not done?
Why stand I tampering midst the listening winds?
My fears are lying traitors.

[Bells at a distance.

Wedding bells,
Thanks for your merry voices; ye have waked
A sudden hurry round about my heart,
I'll think it joy. Now for my second bride.

[Exit.

SCENE IV

A Saloon in Orlando's Palace

OLIVIA, **VIOLETTA**, **NURSE** and **ATTENDANTS**.

OLIVIA
You keep me long: am I not yet attired?
Have ye not tricked me out enough? In faith,
I am so vain to think I need no more.

ATTENDANT
One moment, madam;
This little necklace, like the marriage yoke
Pleasantly binding, I must clasp around you.

OLIVIA
A pretty toy, and prettily disposed;
I have, I know not why, this livelong day
Wept drops enough to bead a thousand such.
Where's Violetta? Come, look up, my girl,
Make thine eyes sparkle; mine are very moist.

VIOLETTA
Shake off this sadness, lady, 'tis not meet
At such a moment; think upon your bridegroom,
How his affections seek thee.

OLIVIA

Gentle maid,
I'll not be sad; yet, little Violet,
How long I've worn thy beauty next my heart,
Aye, in my very thoughts, where thou hast shed
Perpetual summer: how long shared thy being:
Like two leaves of a bud, we've grown together,
And needs must bleed at parting.

VIOLETTA

No, not so;
I am thy handmaid still; and when your lord
Is absent, as he will be, at the tourney,
The court, or camp, we'll drive the long hours on
With prattle as of old.

OLIVIA

Thanks, I'll be cheerful;
But joy's a plant the showers of many sorrows
Must water, ere it bloom. Good nurse, your pardon,
You've known me for a forward child before.

NURSE

Now, on the scanty remnant of my life,
Grief's an ill wedding garment; if you'd put
One of your rosy smiles on, what a grace
You'd look and be. Why, all these ohs and sobs
Are more like funeral noises.

OLIVIA

'Troth they are,
And 'tis the funeral of that Olivia
You nursed and knew; an hour and she's no more,
No more the mistress of her own resolves,
The free partaker of earth's airs and pleasures;
My very love, the poorest gift I have,
(Which, light as 'tis, I thought you all did prize,)
Is not my own. We must be strangers, girls;
Give me your hands and wishes.

NURSE

There is one,
Old now, and withered, truly we might call it
Yours, and not mine; oft has it brought you food,
Led you, and served you; yet in gladness parts
To make way for a younger and a worthier.

OLIVIA

My kind old nurse; nay, now you are forgetting
Your words of cheer; this hand shall never want
Aid while I live, your service will be needful;
My house would seem a strange and dismal place
Without your pleasant looks.

NURSE
Well, my dear child,
I hope you'll give my arms a new Olivia;
Blush not; the old will talk.

OLIVIA
Whose hand is this
I know not from my own? Young Violet's?
My beauteous innocence, you must be with me
Oft, as you said: Go to, my nurse forbids
Our weeping.

VIOLETTA
Don't chide me then, Olivia,
I'm a sad fool, but do not chide.

OLIVIA
A gem
For Friendship's crown, each drop. My loving maids,
To each a farewell that I cannot speak;
All have my heart, and well can read its meaning.
Henceforth I'll look upon my maiden years
As lovely pastoral pictures; all of you
Shall smile again 'neath Memory's wizard pencil;
The natural beauties that we've marked together
Will look you back again; the books we've loved
Will talk to me of your sweet-worded praises,
The air of our old haunts whisper your voices;
Trust me, I'll not forget you.

ATTENDANT
Dearest lady,
May all the blessings that rain down from heaven
Upon the marriage-bed, descend on yours;
May many children, innocent and fair,
With soft embracements throng about your knees,
Domestic pleasures ever turn your hour-glass,
And, when the long sleep falls upon your eyes,
Content and holy Peace, the twins of Eden,
Draw round the curtain 'twixt you and the world,
And watch beside you all the dreary night.

SCENE V

A Room in Mordred's Cottage

Enter **LENORA** supporting **MORDRED**.

MORDRED
Here let me rest, in my old oaken chair:
My limbs grow faint, and yet, kind, careful nurse,
Your smiles have chased away my pains.

LENORA
Dear husband,
A thousand thanks for those delightful words;
They bid me hope again and warm my heart.

MORDRED
It renovates the spirit thus to look,
With the clear eye of health and joyousness,
Upon the green creation. But I miss
A smile of hope, the copy of Lenora's,
That's wont to light my soul with its rich love;
Where is my peach-cheeked girl, my Floribel?

LENORA
She will be with us soon; before you woke,
She went to ramble underneath the boughs,
And feed her forest birds; each bower she knows
Of eglantine and hawthorn; now the air
Is calm, she will return.

MORDRED
I hope she may;
Yet who could injure such a holy thing?
The frenzied tempest's self, had it a will,
Would leave her path secure. My dear Lenora,
There is one thing I wish to see accomplished
Before I die.

LENORA
What is it, love? And yet methinks 'twere fit
For me still to defer its execution,
And cheat you into living to that end.

MORDRED
Long have I prayed to see her beauty growing

Under some worthy husband's firm protection.

LENORA
What if she be already wedded?

MORDRED
No,
That cannot be, she would have told unto me
The first emotions of her infant love;
She never had a thought concealed from me,
Even her slightest. 'Tis impossible;
And yet you look in earnest; speak, and tell me
You only jest.

LENORA
I speak indeed the truth;
Perhaps I was imprudent not to tell you,
But you were very ill, and, such the match,
You could not disapprove: Young Hesperus—

MORDRED
Lord Ernest's son!

LENORA
The same.

MORDRED
I'm satisfied,
My wish is all fulfilled. There's not a man
Beneath the sun more noble; but his father
Was wont to be a stern imperious lord,
A scorner of the poor.

LENORA
He did not know it.

MORDRED
He knew it not! That was a sad omission,
Unworthy of a parent; we might rue it.

LENORA
This night our daughter's bridegroom
Comes, as his own to claim her, and, ere this,
Doubtless has told the love-tale to his father.

MORDRED
I wish him speedy, he shall find a welcome,
In the poor man's sole wealth, my hearty love.

Hark! There's a step.

LENORA
'Tis Hesperus'; I know it.

[Enter the **HUNTSMAN**.

MORDRED
Who comes, who is it?

LENORA
One, whose visage wears
The darkest sadness; such a man I'd choose
For the mute herald of disaster.

HUNTSMAN
Lady,
Would that my looks could mirror to your soul
The woe, each syllable of which in speaking
Tears through my heart. Alas! your lovely daughter—

LENORA
What? Speak I pray thee. Has she met with aught?

MORDRED
Bid me die, or my fears.

[Enter **HUBERT** with the body of **FLORIBEL**.

HUNTSMAN
Here's all that's left
Of nature's rarest work: this lifeless all.
Oh! fall some strange, unheard-of punishment
On Hesperus' head.

MORDRED
Hesperus, Hesperus; oh!

[Falls back in his chair.

HUBERT
Aye, 'twas his hand that wrought its passage here,
And murdered love in its most sacred temple.

[**LENORA** takes the body into her lap and sits nursing it.

HUNTSMAN
Alas! he heeds not; he is with his daughter.

Look at this other.

HUBERT
Oh! I cannot bear it;
Leave her, a mother's agony is holy
As nature's mysteries.

HUNTSMAN
We'll to the Duke,
And crush the viper in his nest, before
Report alarm him. Gently, gently tread
And wake not echo in this home of woe.

[Exeunt **HUBERT** and the **HUNTSMAN**.

LENORA [Sings in a distracted manner]
Lullaby, lullaby, sweet be thy sleep!
Thou babe of my bosom, thou babe of my love;
Close, close to my heart, dear caresser, you creep,
And kiss the fond eyelid that watches above.

One touch of those warm lips and then to bed.
Where is my child? I held her in my arms,
Her heart was beating in my bosom. Ha!
It is not she that lies upon my breast,
It is not she that whispers in my ear,
It is not she that kisses my salt cheek;
They've stolen her from my couch and left this changeling,
Men call Despair—and she it is I suckle.
I know her by her killing lips of snow,
Her watery eye-balls and her tear-swoll'n cheeks.
My Floribel! oh they have ta'en her soul
To make a second spring of it, to keep
The jarring spheres in melody. Come, husband,
We'll wander up and down this wintry world,
And, if we see a sadder sight than this,
Or hear a tale, though false, of half such horror,
We'll closely hug our bosom-griefs in transport.
Why, husband! You're asleep—you're deaf—you're dead!
I have not eyes enough to weep for both,
But I'll go steal the sleeping world's, and beg
A little dew from every sipping worm
To wet my cheeks with.

SCENE I

An Apartment in Orlando's Palace

HESPERUS alone.

HESPERUS
How now? This quaint attire of countenance,
(Well fitted by prim Conscience's old tailor,
Hypocrisy,) sits rarely, and I'm here,
The affable, good bridegroom. Wickedness,
How easy is thy lesson! Now I stand
Up to the throat in blood; from Mercy's records
For evermore my guilty name is rased.
But yesterday, oh blessed yesterday,
I was a man;
And now—I start amazed at myself.
This hand, aye this it was I gave to Sin,
His grasp hath blasted it; 'twas made for kindness,
For gentle salutation, to deal out
Merciful alms; confirm the staff of age;
To reach the crust to want, the balm to sickness,
And balsam wounds; a limb of charity.
Now the wild adder's sting, the lightning's edge,
Are blunt and tame and gentle to it. Psha!
Why then, men dread the adder and the flash;
So shall they cringe to me. A step! In haste
I've washed, and thought me spotless. Yet I fear
Mine eye is so familiarized with blood,
It doth pass o'er and disregard the stains:
That recks not. Sure I've brushed away those blushes,
And shaken hesitation from my tongue.

[Enter **ATTENDANT**.

Menial, you're hasty in intruding thus.
Your errand?

ATTENDANT
Lady Olivia—

HESPERUS
Give me thine hand. That name
Makes him my friend, who speaks it. Say't again;
Olivia, oh! how each sweet syllable
Trickles along the tongue, an honied drop
Of harmony, Olivia. I'll give all
The yellow wretchedness of human wealth

Unto the subtle artist, who shall teach
A clock to tell the seconds by that word;
So shall I drive these frightful thoughts away,
And happiness—Do I look happy, sirrah?
It matters not. Speak on.

ATTENDANT
My lord, your bride—

HESPERUS
Well sir, it was not I; why lookest thou so?
Beware. Why layest thine hand across thy breast?
Is there a wound on't? Say.

ATTENDANT
A wound, my lord!
I understand not—

HESPERUS
Fool, I know thou dost not.
(If they would find it out, why let them dig
To hell's foundations.)   What! Because I fold
Mine arms like any man unhurt, unhurting,
Must every slave suppose 'tis to conceal
Some fearful witness of a deed?

ATTENDANT
I thought not
'Twould anger thee; forgive me.

HESPERUS
Be it so;
It was too warmly said, for, as I trust,
You could not deem your master villain; never.
Yet say it were so, I but say suppose,
That I, whose clay is kneaded up with tears,
Had murdered, as you thought, some kindred creature;
Could not I wash the tokens of my guilt
From this outside, and show a hand as clean
As he who fingers first the air?

ATTENDANT
You might,
Till heaven's justice blasted you, be hid:
But leave these strange and ugly arguments;
The very fear would scare me from your side;
So banish them.

HESPERUS

Ay, they are strange indeed;
But mirth, believe me, mirth. Come, tell me now,
How sits this ring? Death! are your eyes nailed there?
Ha! Does the ruby cast a sanguine shade
Across the veins?

ATTENDANT

Nought, save the splendid gem,
Amazed my sight; that's all.

HESPERUS

My friend, 'tis thine,
Too poor a recompense for the good tidings
Your tongue is laden with; now speak them out.

ATTENDANT

First let me bless you for your bounty, sir.
I came to call you to the wedding train,
Which waits without; such smiles, on such rare faces,
Mine eyes have never seen: the bride is there;
None but yourself is wanting to perfect
This sum of joy.

HESPERUS

Say I'll be there anon;
And, mark me, on thy life forget each word
I just have spoken, blot them utterly
Out of thy mind; I can reward a service.
I like thee well, my trusty, pleasant friend;
Nay, pr'ythee go, there is no need of thanks.

[Exit **ATTENDANT**.

I'll give that fellow's blab-tongue to the worms,
He's heard too much; 'twere well to call him back,
And fasten down his memory with a dagger.
No, I'll not soil my skin again to-day;
Down, Murder, down!
These untamed passions, that I keep about me,
Will thrive on nought save blood; but they must fast,
And wear a specious tameness. My Olivia,
How my whole soul is thine,—thine and the fiends'.

[Exit.

The Interior of the Duke's Palace

Enter the **DUKE**, **HUBERT** and the **HUNTSMAN**.

DUKE
Your tale hath stunned me with its dreadful import,
And turned my every faculty to wonder.

HUBERT
You cannot doubt, my liege?

DUKE
Hubert, I'd give
The best part of my power for hope to whisper
A no to my conviction. Devilish villain!

HUBERT
Sure all good angels looked another way,
When this foul deed was done.

DUKE
All ancient cruelties
Look pale to it, and merciful: henceforth
They, that would christen human fiends, must write
Hesperus, 'stead of Cain; and chiding nurses,
To still their peevish babes, shall offer them,
Not to the wolves, but him, the fiercer beast.

HUBERT
Oh! my good lord, even now my sight is dimmed
With the salt gush, that came between my eyes
And that which seared them: on her turfy couch,
Like one just lulled into a heavy sleep,
Smiling and calm she lay; the breath
Had not left fluttering up and down her bosom,
That, all blood-dabbled and besprent with gore,
Still held the guilty steel; the name was on it
Of the cursed owner.

DUKE
Go, trusty Hubert,
Speed to Orlando's palace with my guard,
And drag the murderer here; e'en now I'll judge him:
Be diligent, put wings upon your feet;
Some vengeance will fall on us in the night,
If he remain unsentenced.

[Exeunt.

A Banqueting Hall

LORD ERNEST, ORLANDO, CLAUDIO, OLIVIA, VIOLETTA, LORDS, LADIES and **ATTENDANTS.**

LORD ERNEST
Sit here, my daughter; sit and welcome, all;
You shall not say my Hesperus' nuptial night
Lacks its due orgies.

CLAUDIO
Look upon the bride,
How blushes open their envermeiled leaves
On her fair features.

LORD ERNEST
Sit, I pray you, sirs,
We will have deep and jovial carousal;
Put on the smiles of joy, and think of nought
But present pleasure, we've had woes enough;
Bid 'em be merry, daughter.

OLIVIA
Gentlemen,
My father wills me give you all a welcome,
And, if you love or honour our poor house,
Be glad with us.

CLAUDIO
We thank your courtesy, lady, and obey.

LORD ERNEST
Where is this dilatory bridegroom still?
He was not wont to lag; what hast thou done
To banish him, Olivia?

OLIVIA
Good, my lord,
I fear his heart is ill. A veil of gloom
Darkens his cheeks, an anxious watchfulness
Plays in his eyes; and, when he clasped my hand
Now in the chapel, though he smiled and whispered

Of bliss and love, an ague thrilled his veins,
And starting back he groaned.

LORD ERNEST
Go, fetch him hither,
I warrant wine will cure him.

ATTENDANT
Here he comes.

[Enter **HESPERUS**.

HESPERUS [aside]
What's all this blaze and riot? Oh, a banquet.
They should have got me here the seven sins,
And all the evil things that haunt the world;
Then what a goodly revel would we hold;
E'en Death, while hastening to the sick man's pillow,
Should pause to listen our unhallowed talk,
And think us all the brood of Pestilence
Met in mysterious council.

ATTENDANT
Sir, your father
Has been enquiring for you, and desires
The comfort of your presence at the table.

HESPERUS
The comfort of my presence! Slave, thou mockest me.
Why dost thou thrust thy taper in my face?
No price is set on't.

LORD ERNEST
Hither, Hesperus;
Thou dost not mark this company of kinsmen,
Met to congratulate you, and partake
Your gladness.

HESPERUS
Sirs, I thank you heartily.
[aside]
A curse upon the gaping saucy rabble;
They must stare too.

LORD ERNEST
Come, son, and sit beside me;
They say you're ill, my boy.

HESPERUS

They say the truth.

LORD ERNEST

What is your ailment?

HESPERUS

Life. But here is one
Born to smile misery out of the world:
Look on me, my Olivia.

OLIVIA

Dearest Hesperus,
Be calmer, I beseech you; all are here
My friends, and yours.

HESPERUS

No doubt. They drain our goblets.
A friend! What is't? A thing shall squeeze your hand,
Caress with fervent love your broidered sleeve,
And wring his mouth into a leering lie,
While his heart damns thee. One whose love's as deep
As your gold coffer. Hast a wife? They come;
Buz, buz, lie, lie, the hungry meat-flies come,
"Dear lord, sweet lord, our only gentle lord!"
Ay, thus they sugar o'er the silent dagger,
And love, and love, till they've inhelled thy soul.
Oh! when I call for friend, bring honest poison.
Put out the lights, I like the beams o' th' moon;
And tell those revellers to tope in silence.

LORD ERNEST

You would not overcast our best-meant mirth,
Bid us sit palled, like mourners at your bridal,
And hide in night our kindly countenances?

HESPERUS

Ay, by my grave I would. There is on earth
One face alone, one heart, that Hesperus needs;
'Twere better all the rest were not. Olivia,
I'll tell thee how we'll 'scape these prying eyes;
We'll build a wall between us and the world,
And, in some summer wilderness of flowers,
As though but two hearts beat beneath the sun,
Consume our days of love.

LORD ERNEST

I pray you, friends,

Excuse the wilful boy, his soul is wholly
Wrapt up in admiration of his bride:
We'll have her health; come, fill your goblets round,
The bride, Olivia.

CLAUDIO
Happiness befall her,
May she ne'er feel a woe; we drink to her.

[Music.

[Enter **HUBERT**.

HUBERT
Hush, hush; ye ill-timed sounds, let darkness come,
And with her funeral trappings hang the walls,
Or twilight lend a weak and fitful gleam,
That you way watch each others' watery cbeeks.
Oh! ladies, deck your beauties with salt diamonds,
Wail with the midnight wind, and look as sad
As if ye heard the thunder-voice of doom.

LORD ERNEST
What art thou, fearful man?

HUBERT
Woe's harbinger;
I come to bid you to a funeral;
Prepare your eyes, for they must see dire vengeance
Fall on the neck of crime.

HESPERUS
Turn out that fellow;
I know him for a crazy marvel-monger,
A long-faced gossip, with his batch of wonders:
And now he'll tell you the most terrible news,
How many owls and ravens screeched last night,
Or how some ghost has left his marble tomb
To blab a drunken lie.

HUBERT
I tell a fiend
His guilt is hid no more. Ho! there, the guard:

[Enter **GUARDS**.

That is your prisoner.

HESPERUS
You tread a scorpion:
The first that stirs brings to my sword his heart;
Ye plunge into your graves.

[The **GUARDS** seize him.

Ah! Floribel;
Thou draggest my steel away, thou'st frozen me:
Girl, thou art pale.

LORD ERNEST
How's this?
Ruffians, where do you bear my boy? Release him,
Or I'll—

OLIVIA
Oh! do not anger them. They're men
Who have sucked pity from their mothers' breasts,
They will not close their ears to my petition;
And, if they'll loose him, I will pray for them
While speech is mine.

LORD ERNEST
Your swords, my friends, your swords.

HUBERT
Stand back, my lords; let the Duke's prisoner pass.

LORD ERNEST
The Duke! what Duke dare seize my Hesperus?
My noble friends, my—sheath your coward swords,
And put your eyes upon the ground for fear,
Your Jove, the Duke he said;—hear ye no thunder?
But all the warriors of the universe
Shall not cow me: I'll free him; villains, back.

HUBERT
Oh! good old man; alas! he is a murderer.

LORD ERNEST
A murderer!

[Drops his sword.

This is a baby's arm.

OLIVIA

Save him, oh save him! I am very faint.

[**ORLANDO**, **VIOLETTA**, and **ATTENDANTS**, carry her out.

HESPERUS
Hence with that voice! So shrieked—I must not think.

HUBERT
Look to Lord Ernest. The Duke sits in council,
Waiting your presence, lords. On, to the palace.

[Exeunt **CLAUDIO**, **HUBERT**, **HESPERUS**, **GUARDS**, **LORDS** and **Ladies**. Manent **LORD ERNEST** and
ATTENDANTS.

LORD ERNEST
Where is he? What! Ye traitors, let him pass,
Chained, guarded? By this light—gird on your swords.
My hairs are grey, but yet I've blood enough—
Did they not speak of crime? These limbs aren't mine,
But some consumptive girl's.—Ay, it was murder!
I'll see the Duke—support me to the palace.

[Exeunt.

SCENE IV

A Street Before the Ducal Palace

TWO GUARDS attending the body of **FLORIBEL**; **LENORA** hanging over it.

1st GUARD
'Tis time to bear the body to the council:
The criminal is there already.

2nd GUARD
Stay;
'Twere sacrilege to shake yon mourner off,
And she will perish in the wintry night,
If unattended: yet this poor dumb witness
Is needful at the trial. While she sleeps
With careful hands convey her to the Duke's,
And bid the women tend her.

1st GUARD
Soft! She breaks
Her trance, and rises like a new-born thing

Fresh from the realm of spirits.

2nd GUARD
Hush! she speaks.

LENORA
I dreamed, and in that visioned agony
'Twas whispered by strange voices, like the deads',
I was the mother of this Floribel,
And still a wanderer upon man's earth;
No, no, I am her ghost, shade of her essence,
Thrust into some strange shape of womanhood
Until the tomb is open. What are these?
Good sir, have you a tear to throw away,
A little sigh to spare unto the wind?
I've heard that there are hearts yet in the world,
Perhaps you have one.

1st GUARD
Lady, for your sorrow
It aches most deeply.

LENORA
Prithee, look you here.
Cold, cold; 'tis all in vain: those lustrous eyes
Will never beam again beneath the stars;
Darkened for ever; and those wan, dead lips:
They'll put her in the earth and let the world,
The pitiless bad world, tread o'er her beauty,
While I—ye airs of heaven, why will ye feed me?
Why, ye officious ministers, bestow
The loathed blessing of a cursed existence?
There's many a one now leans upon the cheek
Of his dead spouse, a-listening for her pulse,
And hears no motion but his bursting heart;
Give him my life and bid him wipe his eyes.
Look here, look here,
I've heard them call her flower; oh! had she been
The frailest rose that whitens in the blast
Thus bruised and rifled by a ruffian hand,
I might have kept her living in my tears
A very little while, until I die;
And then—now tell me this and I will bless thee,
Where thinkest our spirits go?

1st GUARD
Madam, I know not;
Some say they hang like music in the air,

Some that they sleep in flowers of Paradise,
Some that they lie ingirt by cloudy curtains,
Or 'mong the stars.

LENORA
Oh! not among the stars,
For, if she's there, my sight's so dimmed with tears,
I ne'er shall find her out,
But wander through the sparkling labyrinth
Wearied, alone; oh! say not 'mong the stars.
Why do ye move her?

1st GUARD
We must bear her hence
Unto the **DUKE**

LENORA
What! Is it not enough
That she is dead?

1st GUARD
No hand shall offer hurt,
And in short space we'll bring her back again,
Unto your cottage.

LENORA
Thanks! They shall not harm her;
Soldier, I will repay this kindness nobly;
Hark you; I'm going far off, to Paradise,
And if your child, or wife, or brother's there,
I'll bring them to you in your dreams some night.
Farewell; I will go search about for Comfort,
Him, that, enrobed in mouldering cerements, sits
At the grey tombstone's head beneath the yew;
Men call him Death, but Comfort is his name.

[Exeunt.

[Enter **TWO CITIZENS**.

1st CITIZEN
Well met sir, come you from the trial?

2nd CITIZEN
Ay;
In wonder that the stones do not come down
To crush that monster of all wickedness,
The wretched Hesperus; there he stands,

Biting his chains and writhing in his rage
Like a mad tiger.

1st CITIZEN
Is he yet condemned?

2nd CITIZEN
Death is the sentence.

1st CITIZEN
See, the criminal
And his old father; what a sight of pity.

Enter **HESPERUS** guarded, **ORLANDO, HUBERT, LORD ERNEST** and **MOB**.

HESPERUS
Well, gaping idiots; have ye stared enough;
Have ye yet satisfied your pious minds,
By thanking your most bounteous stars ye're not
A prodigy like this? Get home and tell
Your wives, and put me in your tales and ballads;
Get home and live.

LORD ERNEST
Oh hush my son,
Get some good priest of Charity to draw
Tears of repentance from your soul, and wake
The sleeping virtue.

HESPERUS
Who's this greybeard driveller?
Go, find your wits, old fellow, that bald skull
Is full of leaks; hence! look in last night's bowl;
Search all your money-bags: don't come abroad
Again without them; 'tis amiss.

LORD ERNEST
Oh heavens!
Is this the son, over whose sleeping smiles
Often I bent, and, mingling with my prayers
Thanksgivings, blessed the loan of so much virtue.

HESPERUS
That's right; weep on, weep on; for thou art he,
Who slew his only child, his first-born child.

ORLANDO
Oh look upon his galling agony,

These desperate yearnings of paternal love,
And try to have an heart.

HESPERUS
You're merry, friend;
Troth 'tis a goodly jest: what, dost thou think
These limbs, the strength of nature's armoury,
That but exist to dare, and dare the things
That make the blood of bravery turn pale
For very terror, such a minion's work,
The offspring of those dribbling veins? Go to,
Thou'rt a sad idiot.

LORD ERNEST
Oh! hear him not, thou ever-present Justice,
And close thy watchful eyelid, thou that weighest
Th' allotted scale of crime.

HESPERUS
Come hither, age;
I have a whisper for your secrecy;
Consider; who am I?

LORD ERNEST
Thou wast my son,
The pulse of my dead heart, light of my eyes,
But now—

HESPERUS
Thy son! I would I'd time to laugh.
No, no; attend. The night, that gave me being,
There was unearthly glee upon the winds,
There were strange gambols played beneath the moon,
The madman smiled uncouthly in his sleep,
And children shrunk aghast at goblin sights;
Then came a tap against the rattling casement,
Not the owl's wing, or struggle of the blast;
Thy dotardship snored loudly, and meanwhile
An incubus begot me.

LORD ERNEST
Lead me home,
My eyes are dim; I cannot see the way:
I fain would sleep.

[Exit with some of the **CITIZENS**.

HESPERUS

Go, some one, tell his nurse
To get him swaddling clothes.

ORLANDO
Prodigious wretch!
Rebel to man and heaven! On thee shall fall
The cureless torture of the soul, the woe
Hell nurses for the deepest damned.

HESPERUS
'Tis pity
So much good cursing should be thrown away;
Well spit, my reptile! Officers, lead on:
Shall I, in bondage, stand to glut the sight
Of these poor marvel-dealing things? Away,
I'll shut them out; the red death on you all!

[Going.

Ah! my good fellow, are you of the train
That wait upon Olivia?

ATTENDANT
I'm her servant.

HESPERUS
How fares she?

ATTENDANT
Very ill; she wastes,
Careless of living.

HESPERUS
Tell her, on my love
I charge her live; oh heaven, she must not die,
There are enough accusers in the tomb.
Tell her—Shame, shame, they shall not see me weep.

[Exeunt.

ACT V

SCENE I

A Room in Mordred's Cottage

The dead **FLORIBEL** laid upon a couch. **LENORA** and **BOY**.

LENORA
Why dost thou weep, thou little churl?

BOY
Alas!
I need not say.

LENORA
Boy, boy; thou'rt wicked; thou wouldst have me think
I have no Floribel, but thou shalt see
How I will make her live.
It is the morning,
And she has risen to tend her favourite flowers,
And, wearied with the toil, leans o'er her seat
In silent languor. Now I will steal in,
Softly: perchance she sleeps. It's plain she hears not,
Or she would leap all-smiling to my arms;
I wish dear Mordred were awake to see
How the sweet girl will start and welcome me,
At my first speaking: but I'll wait awhile,
And save the pleasure. Ah! thou pretty silence,
I know thou'rt thinking what a happy cot
'Twill be when our loved patient is quite well.
Yes, you shall take him his first walk; he'll lean
Upon that arm, and you shall show the plants
New set in the garden, and the grassy path
Down to the church.
Now I will stand behind her,
So,—she must drop her head upon my bosom,
As she looks up. Good-morrow to thee, sweet;
Now for her gentle cry; she's turning round.
No—for she wont seem startled, but pretend
To have heard my coming. Why art thou so slow?
Sweet little wag, I know thou'rt not asleep.
Soft! 'Tis the swiftness of my thought outruns
Her proper motions. I've this instant spoken,
The air has scarcely yet ta'en up my words;
May be she hears not. But I did not speak;
'Twas only thought, or whispered. Child, good-morrow;
Yes, she hears that, but will not stir even yet.
I'll not be frightened, for she surely hears;
Though, if I had not seen her garments move,
And caught the tiny echo of her breath,
'Twere dreadful. Speak, I pray thee, Floribel,
Speak to thy mother; do but whisper "ay;"
Well, well, I will not press her; I am sure

She has the welcome news of some good fortune,
And hoards the telling till her father comes;
Perhaps she's found the fruit he coveted
Last night. Ah! she half laughed. I've guessed it then;
Come tell me, I'll be secret. Nay, if you mock me,
I must be very angry till you speak.
Now this is silly; some of those young boys
Have dressed the cushions with her clothes in sport.
'Tis very like her. I could make this image
Act all her greetings; she shall bow her head,
"Good-morrow mother;" and her smiling face
Falls on my neck.—Oh, heaven, 'tis she indeed!
I know it all—don't tell me.

SCENE II

The Interior of a Prison

HESPERUS alone.

HESPERUS
Hark! Time's old iron voice already counts
The steps unto the after-world, o'er which
Sleep in her arms hath carried man to-night;
And all it wakes to business or to joy,
Save one; and, mingled with its solemn tone,
I heard the grating gates of hell expand—
Oh! house of agony,
I feel thy scorching flames already near.
Where shall I 'scape? Is there no hiding place?
Spirit, that guidest the sun, look round this ball,
And through the windows of deep ocean's vault;
Is there no nook just big enough for me?
Or, when I'm dead, can I not pass my soul
For common air, and shroud me in some cloud?
But then the earth will moulder, clouds evanish;
So Hell, I must unto thee, darksome vale;
For dared I hope, I could not wish, Elysium:
There should I meet the frowns of Floribel;
My father would be there:—black gulph of anguish,
Thou art far better than such paradise.
Why did they teach me there is such a place?
The pang of misery is there; I know
There is a land of bliss, and am not in it;
This, this outstings your lashes, torturers;
He has no lack of punishment who feels it.

[Enter **JAILOR**.

Oh! speak not for a moment, speak not, sir,
I know thine errand well; so tell it not.
But let me shut mine eyes, and think a little
That I am what I was. Ay, there he sits,
My good old sire, with his large eye of love.
How well it smiles upon that lovely maid,
A beauteous one, indeed; and yet, they say,
She died most cruelly. Oh! tell me something,
Drive out these dreams.

JAILOR
Prisoner, prepare for death.

[Exit.

HESPERUS
Death! Death! What's death? I cannot think.

[Enter **LENORA**.

Who art thou?

LENORA
Ha! knowest thou not the wretch thou'st made Lenora?
Alone I've found thee, villain.

HESPERUS
Not alone;
Oh! not alone: the world hath burst its ribs,
And let out all the demons in the pit;
Thick; thick they throng: I cannot breathe for them;
The hounds of Lucifer are feeding on me,
Yet I endure; Remorse and Conscience too,
Stirring the dying embers of my heart,
Which Passion hath burnt out, like midnight gossips
Sit idly chattering of the injured dead;
But thou'rt the last and worst; I hoped to hide
Beneath the turf from thee.

LENORA
Thou shalt not leave me; stand and hear my curse,—
Oh such a curse! I learned it from a voice
That wandered 'mid the damned: it burns my tongue,
Listen, wretch, listen;
Thus, thus I curse thee.......No I do revoke it,

My pardon be upon you for your deeds;
Though thou didst stab me through my Floribel,
I think thou once didst love her; didst thou not?

HESPERUS
With my whole soul, as now I worship her.

LENORA
Alas! say no; I wish thou'dst break my heart;
Now, pr'ythee do; I'll bless thee for't again.

HESPERUS
What! is it stubborn yet? Then thou canst teach me
How to bear misery—but I need it not,
They've dug my grave.

LENORA
But, while you still are living,
What say you to some frolic merriment?
There are two grassy mounds beside the church,
My husband and my daughter; let us go
And sit beside them, and learn silence there;
Even with such guests we'll hold our revelry
O'er bitter recollections: there's no anguish,
No fear, no sorrow, no calamity,
In the deathful catalogue of human pains,
But we will jest upon't, and laugh and sing:
Let pitiful wretches whine for consolation,
Thank heaven we despair.

[Enter **GUARDS**.

HESPERUS
See you these men?
They bid me to a strange solemnity.

LENORA
Must thou be gone?

HESPERUS
I must, alas! for ever.
Live and be blessed, mother of Floribel.

[Exit with **GUARDS**.

LENORA
Farewell; farewell. They drag him to the scaffold,
My son, the husband of my Floribel:

They shall not slaughter him upon the block,
And to the cursing multitude hold up
The blackened features which she loved; they shall not.

[Exit.

SCENE III

An Apartment in Orlando's Palace

OLIVIA, **VIOLETTA**, and **ATTENDANTS**.

OLIVIA
Sing me that strain, my gentle Violet,
Which erst we used, in sport and mockery
Of grief, beneath the willow shade at eve
To chaunt together; 'twill allay my woes.

SONG, by TWO VOICES

FIRST VOICE
Who is the baby, that doth lie
Beneath the silken canopy
Of thy blue eye?

SECOND VOICE
It is young Sorrow, laid asleep
In the crystal-deep.

BOTH VOICES
Let us sing his lullaby,
Heigho! a sob and a sigh.

FIRST VOICE
What sound is that, so soft, so clear,
Harmonious as a bubbled tear
Bursting, we hear?

SECOND VOICE
It is young Sorrow, slumber breaking,
Suddenly awaking.

BOTH VOICES
Let us sing his lullaby,
Heigho! a sob and a sigh.

OLIVIA

'Tis well: you must not weep; 'twill spoil your voices,
And I shall need them soon.

VIOLETTA

For what, Olivia?
You were not wont to prize our simple skill
Erewhile so highly: what will please you most?
What lay of chivalry, or rural sport,
Or shepherd love, shall we prepare you next?

OLIVIA

My dirge: I shall not tax your music else.
It must be: wherefore weep?

VIOLETTA

I cannot help it,
When you converse so mournfully of death;
You must forgive me.

OLIVIA

Death! thou silly girl,
There's no such thing; 'tis but a goblin word,
Which bad men conjure from their reeking sins
To haunt their slumbers; 'tis a life indeed.
These bodies are the vile and drossy seeds,
Whence, placed again within their kindred earth,
Springs Immortality, the glorious plant
Branching above the skies. What is there here
To shrink from? Though your idle legends tell
How cruelly he treats the prostrate world;
Yet, unto me, this shadowy potentate
Comes soft and soothing as an infant's sleep,
And kisses out my being. Violetta,
Dost thou regard my wish, perhaps the last?

VIOLETTA

Oh! madam, can you doubt it? We have lived
Together ever since our little feet
Were guided on the path, and thence have shared
Habits and thoughts. Have I in all that time,
That long companionship, e'er thwarted thee?
Why dost thou ask me then? Indeed I know not
Thy wishes from my own, but to prefer them.
Then tell me what you will; if its performance
But occupy the portion of a minute,
'Twill be a happy one, for which I thank you.

OLIVIA

Thine hand upon it; I believe thy promise.
When I am gone you must not weep for me,
But bring your books, your paintings, and your flowers,
And sit upon my grassy monument
In the dewy twilight, when they say souls come
Walking the palpable gross world of man,
And I will waft the sweetest odours o'er you;
I'll shower down acorn-cups of spicy rain
Upon your couch, and twine the boughs above;
Then, if you sing, I'll take up Echo's part,
And from a far-off bower give back the ends
Of some remembered airy melody;
Then, if you draw, I'll breathe upon the banks
And freshen up the flowers, and send the birds,
Stammering their madrigals, across your path;
Then, if you read, I'll tune the rivulets,
I'll teach the neighbouring shrubs to fan your temples,
And drive sad thoughts and fevers from your breast;
But, if you sleep, I'll watch your truant sense,
And meet it in the fairy land of dreams
With my lap full of blessings; 'twill, methinks,
Be passing pleasant, so don't weep for me.

VIOLETTA

I fear, Olivia, I'm a selfish creature,
These tears drop not for you, but for myself;
'Tis not that death will have you, but that I
Shall be a lone lost thing without your love.

OLIVIA

My love will spread its wings for ever near you;
Each gentler, nobler, and diviner thought
Will be my prompting.

VIOLETTA

Well, I'll bear it then,
And even persuade myself this intercourse
Of disembodied minds is no conjecture,
No fiction of romance. The summer sun
Will find me on the sod that covers you,
Among the blossoms; I'll try not to cry;
And when I hear a rustle in the grass,
Or the soft leaves come kissing my bent arm,
I shall not lay it to the empty air,
But think I know thy utterance in the noises
That answer me, and see thy rosy fingers
Dimpling the brooks.

OLIVIA
Thou wilt be cheerful, then?

VIOLETTA
Yes, with this hope,
That when, some silent, melancholy night,
I've sobbed myself to sleep over your picture,
Or some memorial of your former kindness,
I shall awaken to ethereal music,
And find myself a spirit with Olivia.

[A bell tolls.

OLIVIA
Whose summons loads the gale with mournful sound?

ATTENDANT
Dear lady?

OLIVIA
I ask who's dead or who's to die:
You need not tell me: I remember now,—
It was a thought I wished to keep away.
My love, my Hesperus, unto me thou wert
The gentlest and the kindest; sudden madness
Must have inspired this deed; and why do I,
Wife of the dying, tarry in the world?
I feel already dissolution's work;
A languor creeps through all my torpid veins;
Support me, maidens.

VIOLETTA
Come unto your couch;
Sleep will recruit thee.

OLIVIA
Yes; the breathless sleep;
Come and pray round me, as I fade away;
My life already oozes from my lips,
And with that bell's last sound I shall expire.

[Exeunt.

SCENE IV

HESPERUS guarded, **HUBERT**, **ORLANDO**, **CITIZENS** &c.

HESPERUS
Now in the scornful silence of your features
I see my hated self; my friends, I was
The pestilence you think of; but to-night
Angelic ministers have been with me,
And by the holy communings of conscience
Wrought a most blessed change; my soul has wept
And lain among the thorns of penitence;
I ask, (and you will not refuse the boon
To one who cannot crave again) forgiveness
For all that in the noontide of my crimes,
Against you, even in thought, I have committed.

ORLANDO
And we rejoice to grant it; and if prayers,
In meek sincerity outpoured, avail,
You have them from our hearts.

HESPERUS
Thy sister's soul spake in those words, Orlando;
A wretch's blessing for them. I'm as one
In some lone watch-tower on the deep, awakened
From soothing visions of the home he loves;
Trembling he hears the wrathful billows whoop,
And feels the little chamber of his life
Torn from its vale of clouds, and, as it falls,
In his midway to fate, beholds the gleam
Of blazing ships, some swallowed by the waves,
Some, pregnant with mock thunder, tossed abroad,
With mangled carcases, among the winds;
And the black sepulchre of ocean, choaked
With multitudinous dead; then shrinks from pangs,
Unknown but destined. All I know of death
Is, that 'twill come. I have seen many die
Upon the battle field, and watched their lips
At the final breath, pausing in doubt to hear
If they were gone. I have marked oftentimes
Their pale eyes fading in the last blue twilight;
But none could speak the burning agony,
None told his feelings. I ne'er dreamed I died,
Else might I guess the torture that attends it.
But men unhurt have lost their several senses,
Grown deaf, and blind, and dumb without a pang,
And surely these are members of the soul,

And, when they fail, man tastes a partial death:
Besides our minds share not corporeal sleep,
But go among the past and future, or perhaps
Inspire another in some waking world,
And there's another death.
I will not fear; why do ye linger, guards?
I've flung my doubts away; my blood grows wild.

HUBERT
The hour appointed is not yet arrived,
Some moments we must wait; I pray you, patience.

[Enter **LORD ERNEST** in the dress of a peasant, followed by **CLAUDIO**.

CLAUDIO
My lord, where dost thou hurry?

LORD ERNEST
To Despair;
Away! I know thee not. Henceforth I'll live
Those bitter days that Providence decrees me,
In toil and poverty. Oh son, loved son,
I come to give thee my last tear and blessing;
Thou wilt not curse the old, sad wretch again?

HESPERUS [Falling upon the ground and covering himself with the loose earth]
Oh trample me to dust.

LORD ERNEST [Lying down beside him]
My own dear child;
Ay, we will lie thus sweetly in the grave,
(The wind will not awake us, nor the rain,)
Thou and thy mother and myself; but I,
Alas! I have some tearful years to come,
Without a son to weep along with me.

HESPERUS
Father, dear father!
And wilt thou pray for me? Oh, no! thou canst not,
Thou must forget or hate me.

LORD ERNEST
Sirs, have pity;
Let him not use me thus. Hesperus, Hesperus,
Thou'rt going to thy mother; tell her, son,
My heart will soon be broken; so prepare
To have me with you. Bless thee, boy, good night.

[Exit.

HESPERUS
My father, heaven will curse thee if I bless;
But I shall die the better for this meeting.

[Kneeling.

Oh, Floribel! fair martyr of my fury,
Oh, thou blessed saint! look down and see thy vengeance,
And, if thy injured nature still can pity,
Whisper some comfort to my soul. 'Tis done;
I feel an airy kiss upon my cheek;
It is her breath; she hears me; she descends;
Her spirit is around me. Now I'll die.

[Enter **LENORA**.

LENORA
Where's Hesperus? Not gone? Speak to me loud,
I hear not for the beating of my heart.
We're not both dead? Say thou hast 'scaped the headsman,
Nor felt the severing steel fall through thy neck.

HESPERUS
I stay one moment for the signal here,
The next I am no more.

LENORA
Then we have conquered.
Friend, leave us: I would speak a private word
Unto thy prisoner. Look upon these flowers;
They grew upon the grave of Floribel,
And, when I pulled them, through their tendrils blew
A sweet soft music, like an angel's voice.
Ah! there's her eye's dear blue; the blushing down
Of her ripe cheek in yonder rose; and there
In that pale bud, the blossom of her brow,
Her pitiful round tear; here are all colours
That bloomed the fairest in her heavenly face;
Is't not her breath?

HESPERUS [smelling them]
It falls upon my soul
Like an unearthly sense.

LENORA
And so it should,

For it is Death thou'st quaffed:
I steeped the plants in a magician's potion,
More deadly than the scum of Pluto's pool,
Or the infernal brewage that goes round
From lip to lip at wizards' mysteries;
One drop of it, poured in a city conduit,
Would ravage wider than a year of plague;
It brings death swifter than the lightning shaft.

HESPERUS
'Tis true: I feel it gnawing at my heart,
And my veins boil as though with molten lead.
How shall I thank thee for this last, best gift?

LENORA
What is it rushes burning through my mouth?
Oh! my heart's melted.—Let me sit awhile.

HUBERT
Hear ye the chime? Prisoner, we must be gone;
Already should the sentence be performed.

HESPERUS
On! I am past your power.
[To **LENORA**]
How farest thou now?

LENORA
Oh! come with me, and view
These banks of stars, these rainbow-girt pavilions,
These rivulets of music—hark, hark, hark!
And here are winged maidens floating round,
With smiles and welcomes; this bright beaming seraph
I should remember; is it not—my daughter?

[Dies.

HESPERUS
I see not those; but the whole earth's in motion;
I cannot stem the billows; now they roll:
And what's this deluge? Ah! Infernal flames!

[Falls.

HUBERT
Guards, lift him up.

HESPERUS

The bloody hunters and their dogs! Avaunt—
Tread down these serpents' heads. Come hither, Murder;
Why dost thou growl at me? Ungrateful hound!
Not know thy master? Tear him off! Help! Mercy!
Down with your fiery fangs!—I'm not dead yet.

[Dies.

Thomas Lovell Beddoes – A Concise Bibliography

The Comet (The London Morning Post. July 15, 1819)
The Improvisatore (1821)
The Brides' Tragedy (1822)
The Romance of the Lily (The Album, August 1823)
A translation of Schiller's Philosophic Letters (Oxford Quarterly Magazine, June 1825)

Posthumous Publications

Death's Jest-Book, or the Fool's Tragedy (1850)
The Poems, posthumous and collected, of Thomas Lovell Beddoes (2 volumes, 1851)
The Poetical Works of Thomas Lovell Beddoes (1890. With Memoir)
The Letters of Thomas Lovell Beddoes (1894)

www.ingramcontent.com/pod-product-compliance
Lightning Source LLC
Chambersburg PA
CBHW021938040426
42448CB00008B/1128